——INSIDE——
STANFORD
—ADMISSIONS—

Daniel Wu

Andrew Yang

Contents

Hi, please read me.. 1

Some Strategic Thoughts.. 3

Long Essays 7

The Personal Essay... 8

Intellectual Vitality... 33

Roommate Letter.. 45

What is Meaningful 57

Short Essays...69

Significant Challenge... 70

Last Two Summers... 74

Historical Moment 78

Five Words 81

Read, Listen, and Watch.. 83

Looking Forward To Stanford.................................... 89

An Extra Hour 92

Elaborate on an Extracurricular 95

Profiles 99

Essay Sets...167

Against All Odds.. 168

The Academic Powerhouse 220

Cultural Catalysts 276

Conclusion 327

Hi, please read me.

Who are we?

We're current Stanford undergrads who thought college admissions sucked, and wondered if we could see what Stanford said about us. Turns out we can. So we did. After sharing this secret with a bunch of our friends, we decided to collect a bunch of stories, essays, and comments together, and share them with you—getting you *Inside Stanford Admissions*.

In this book, we wanted to give you three things:

1. Examples—real, unedited, writing by students who got in; the good, the bad, and the ugly.

2. Feedback—the raw comments written by Stanford admissions officers on each student file.

3. Advice—our perspectives on what we've just gone through, and what you're about to go through.

How did we do it?

The Family Educational Rights and Privacy Act (FERPA), allows, amongst other things, college students to see what admissions officers wrote about them. We organized 30 current Stanford students in the class of 2022 and 2023 to file FERPA requests with the Registrar's office. Each student was allowed to view copies of their records and comments, but not allowed to take the record with them; instead, we copied down the comments word-for-word.

Do you have disclaimers?

Yup, we do. We printed exactly what comments the students disclosed to us, and did not verify the comments with Stanford. Yes—this means we left in all the horrendous typos, abbreviations, and redactions. Sentence fragments abound. Comments can be fragmented and rudimentary, misremembered or misquoted. Essays were also redacted to protect our contributors.

We hope that this book will help you get inside the mind of a reader; and that the profiles we've included will inspire you, the writer. See you around on campus!

Some Strategic Thoughts

There's plenty of advice out there, so we'll keep it short. Here's some (hopefully unconventional, and interesting) thoughts on applying to college, that we, having just gone through it, have jotted down.

On Your Story

Step one: figure out your story. It should be a one-sentence summary of ~~what you want Stanford to think~~ who you are, and who you'll become. *I'm the endlessly caring doctor-to-be who will bring lifesaving technologies from bench to bedside. I'm the inner-city warrior who will wage a crusade against xenophobia. I'm the soft-hearted jock who will touch hearts and minds on the field.* Write that sentence down.

Once you have that sentence, think about experiences you've had that resonate. Where did you discover your passion? How have you pursued that passion? Examples that stand out in your mind, that convince you, will convince your readers. Those can be the seeds of essays. Write down those anecdotes (no more than 50 words), and keep them in the back of your mind.

Pare down your story. I know, it's painful. You've done a lot. But, unless your story sentence is *"I'm mediocre at everything, but I mean everything,"* you're only exceptional in one or two ways. I'm telling you how it is. So don't distract your reader by talking about your middle school robotics team if you're a lawyer to be, or your summer-long stint at a retirement home if you've switched from premed to econ. You can use that word count in much better ways.

Then, bring it all together. After writing later essays, read your earlier essays to make sure they fit. Once you finish the application, have others give it a look. Then, finally, hit that submit button, relax, and enjoy your senior year.

On Writing

If you're lucky (and responsible) enough to be reading this far before that December deadline, congrats. Read this book, and write down some ideas. But don't write essays yet—instead, let the ideas stew for a while. Your goal is to tell your story in the clearest, most engaging way. Write a bit of each essay at a time. Work on every essay at once. Make them fit together like jigsaw puzzles. Revise, revise, revise, and get feedback (from productive, helpful, people).

If you aren't responsible, and the deadline is tomorrow, good luck. You've probably already written your personal essay (if not, do that first!) and filled out the rest of the Common App. Now, you're thinking about how to write the Stanford application. Some of the questions are, in fact, copy-pastable. The 50 word essays can be banged out in a flash. But the roommate essay is unique; there's not really a similar prompt for any of the other universities. After Frankensteining together the other essays, I'd spend time on that one.

On Admissions Officers

Your admissions officer has a short amount of time to read each essay, but still feels like a sleuth. As such, they read exactly one level deep.

They won't have takeaways like "Wow, this student is really friendly because they wrote 'Everyone really likes me'", or "Wow, this student has had a hard life because they wrote 'My life has been really hard'."

They'll have takeaways like "Hey, the way he phrased that demonstrates his humility," or "Wow, that story really shows how much she's overcome."

They won't have takeaways like "I love how she put all her activity descriptions as haikus, which exemplifies the westernization of the Orient mentioned in her "Biggest Challenge" essay, building on the cultural self-discovery mentioned in her personal essay, which, by the way, was written in iambic pentameter." They'll just think "Oh, that's neat."

Don't underthink it, because they'll read between the lines. Don't overthink it, because the people reading it certainly aren't.

On The Interview

Sorry—I can't teach you EQ. If you're likeable, sociable, and extroverted, you'll probably have tons of fun during the interview. It's an art, not a science—with that being said, take the following scientific suggestions with a grain of salt.

Find out about your interviewer first. At the interview. This means absolutely NO stalking. No Googling, Facebooking, LinkedIn browsing. That information asymmetry is danger-ous—they think you're creepy, and you look bored when they start telling you about themselves. Instead, ask them for their story at the interview, and figure out what you all have in com-mon.

Think about what interviewers are on the watch for ... and on the watch against. Don't be the stuck-up arrogant know-it-all; that's obvious. At the same time, don't be the generic kid who nods and smiles and agrees a lot; they have tons of those inter-views. In short, think about all your friends' personalities who are applying to elite colleges, and imagine what they're like in an interview. Are you puking a little? Don't do those things—it's gross for the interviewer too.

Think about what the interviewer thinks Stanford needs. If your interviewer was class of 1960, before Silicon Valley, their idea of what Stanford is like is probably very different from yours.

Have questions, but not boring ones. Not having a question is better than asking "What was your favorite part about Stan-ford?". You'll immediately get a canned answer that they've given a million times, and they'll get a hazy memory of the interview. Instead, ask about what you've discovered during the interview, about the interviewer. You'll have much more interesting, insightful, conversations that way.

Long Essays

The Personal Essay

The What

Sum up your 18 years of life into ~650 words, to be judged by heartless adults around the nation. Share your passions and dreams, highs and lows, hopes and fears. Be funny but serious, unique but normal, exceptional but growing.

Don't worry, you don't need to do that. In fact, you shouldn't. Don't try to stretch yourself too thin, or touch on everything you've ever done. Instead, sharpen your spike. Use the personal essay to complete your picture, and emphasize where and how you stand out.

The personal essay is the most important thing you write for your college application. It comes in many different forms; on many different applications. This is also one of the toughest things to write, because it's the cornerstone of your application, and something every college will see.

Whether you're writing for the Common Application, the Coalition Application, or the QuestBridge Application, there's a couple things to keep in mind:

Your activities, classes, clubs, and test scores can't be changed, and they've painted a picture of you. What's the biggest thing missing from that picture? What do you want every college to know about you?

Write multiple drafts, and get outside opinions (though certainly not from your parents).

The Why

The real point of the personal essay is to chop out some conceptual space in the admissions officer's head. Trust me, when the officer is looking back at all the files on their desk, they won't remember you as the kid with a 760 on the SAT Math section, but as the underwater basket-weaving kid, the skydiving gymnast kid, the beekeeper kid.

Admissions officers sometimes have 5 minutes per application, to get to know you, and judge you, based on the words you've put to paper. Have a one-sentence story, and drive it home.

The Pitfalls

The best thing you can do is make the reader feel. Laugh. Cry. Gape. Fear. That means you're memorable, and interesting. Build a world through your words—let the reader get a glimpse into your life.

The worst thing you can do is be generic or formulaic. Admissions officers read thousands of essays every year—they've seen it all. Do something *you*—trust me, nobody knows you better than yourself; you're interesting, and your parents, teachers, and guidance counselors are boring, generic, formulaic, writers. Resist the urge to write about something "safe" or "standard," and take the time to think about yourself.

The How

Here's some common questions.

What prompt should I pick?

To be honest, the prompt doesn't matter. They might help guide your thinking, but should probably be ignored. There's usually a wildcard prompt that amounts to "Write about something." — that's the one you pick.

Well, then, what do I write about?

Hey, if I could tell you, I would. Instead, here are some guiding questions:

- How would my best friend introduce me to a stranger?
- What have I been spending my time on this year?
- What location do I spend a lot of time at?
- When my parents want to brag about me to other parents, what do they lead with?
- I'm the only person in my school to have done _____.
- I'm the only person in the world to have done _____.
- Hey! One cool factoid I know is _____.

How do I start?

Words. English, preferably. The starting paragraph should be interesting. You can be interesting by telling a little story, or a joke, or some neat thing about the world. You can wow them with your compositional mastery. The start of your essay should also get your message across. Your message shouldn't be "Let me in," or "Wow, I'm amazing," instead, it should be something along the lines of "I care about _____," or "I am me because _____." Figure out how to get those words across without typing those words on the application.

How much do I brag?

You probably shouldn't lead with your SAT score. Or co-py-paste your activities. I know, I know, it's tempting, but also pretty annoying, if you're a reader. However, if you don't brag, you're missing out on a chance to brag—i.e. reinforce your strong points, and make your application more memorable. One happy medium is to pick one activity or pursuit you feel particularly passionate about, and think about stories, experiences, or takeaways you've had throughout that activity. It's then much easier to work in some of your brag points naturally into your essay, as you'll see below, in our selected samples.

Sample I

"Yeah, I don't really want to go to football today." I slouched in my seat as I informed my parents this would be the end of my football career. My parents' gossip about other parents came to a screeching halt. The silence in my mom's Dodge Caravan was utterly deafening. This was the third sport I had decided was "not for me." This was the third sport that ended in a mind-blowingly painful conversation in the back of that minivan. This was the third sport my parents were convinced I just needed "a few more weeks" to really understand why it was so great. Still, I was convinced all sports were created to punish children. Baseball—intolerably hot. Soccer—too much running. Football—way too aggressive. One factor that undoubtedly led to my distaste for every athletic undertaking was my lack of coordination and skill. The one time I actually scored a touchdown I scored for the wrong team. Moreover, I just knew this was not what I was meant to be doing. I didn't enjoy it. I felt out of place. My parent's enthusiasm for all things sporty fell on deaf ears when they tantalized me with the details of the next sport I could try. But our house was an athletic house. During the week, we played sports. Saturdays were college football. Sundays were professional football. To go against this was to go against my family.

I felt displaced within my family. It felt as if my family and I were on completely different paths that just accidentally crossed paths at the womb. As I grew up, the alienation I felt only grew. Gut-wrenchingly uncomfortable talks about abortion, LGBTQ rights, and healthcare access were eerily reminiscent of those in the back of my mom's minivan.

In high school, I finally found my path. I allowed myself to explore and found things I was passionate about. I joined activities, many of which gave me an idea of who I was as a person. I learned I was a lot better at academics than athletics. I filled my schedule with other activities. Saturdays were Speech & Debate. Sundays were culinary team. And during the week, I worked on DECA. I was determined to show my parents I could still be successful, even without athletics. In a way, I joined these activities in retaliation against my parents' ever-present sports obsession. It was a way to show them—and myself—I could finally be good at something. Because while I had absolutely no chance of ever scoring a touchdown for the right team, maybe, I thought, I could win something else. This ultimately instilled in me a drive to work harder. I felt I had something to prove to my parents. My parents pushed me in a way I did not recognize at the time.

I thought a lot about the disappointed look on my parents' faces when I quit just about every sport imaginable. I was, admittedly, afraid I would see that look again in high school. Instead, I remember vividly when I walked into my house after winning my state championship in DECA and saw the look on my parents' faces. I felt as if they finally understood I was still passionate about something, even if it wasn't athletics. My family and I understood we were different, but we all saw the importance of finding our passions and pushing ourselves to pursue them. Through this, I learned the intrinsicality of our passions, and that parents, try as they may, will never change them. I found my own path; it's radically different from the path my parents might have imagined—and that's okay.

Takeaways

You don't need a "deep", navel-gazing, essay, if you're not a deep, navel-gazing, person.

Why this essay?

This essay "explains" the applicant's activities—painting a picture of a former athlete who found other interests in high school, which resonated better with his interests.

This essay also sets up the central narrative of the rest of his application—being the free-thinker, and the divergent opinion, in a land where his community, and even his family, disagrees with him. Arguing about sports is just a prelude to arguing about broader issues.

How was this essay written?

Oh no—not another sports essay. You can almost hear the groan of the admissions officer. *Is it another torn ACL? One about the "passion for the game"?* Instead, the officer finds something surprising, unique, even genuinely funny. While other applicants might be highlighting their successes, this writer starts with a set of three failures, acknowledging the overbearing nature of their parents, and even makes fun of their own "lack of coordination and skill," and how they "scored a touchdown for the wrong team". That humor is an effective bridge into the central message of ideological rebellion, and the applicant's later transition into other activities, in which he excelled.

What Stanford said

"Ecstatics show deep commitment to DECA and Speech with leadership and participation at state level. PE is a nice musing on finding ones place even when it differs from family culture.

Overall, his writing elevates SPIV for a strong, contemplative voice, a clear curiosity for learning and interest in others."

Concluding remarks

A bread-and-butter essay.

Sample II

Dear all the men in my life,

To my swim coach who pushed me to my limits everyday in and out of the pool: I hope you get your promotion to lead paramedic because you need to continue saving lives, even if it's not in the way you saved mine. You taught me to care for my body and that some numbers, whether race times or weight, will always just be numbers if not motivation.

To the teacher who believed the only fortune I'd ever make was with my body: I hope one day you learn to be as comfortable with female shoulders as the teenage boys who you claim to "worry" for are. You taught me that people will project their insecurities and shortcomings onto others to avoid their fears, like yours of change, and to cover up their feelings of inadequacy, because at 16 I was headed for something bigger than you could ever give me credit for.

To the boy who grabbed me, a delicate sunflower, with careless rough hands that tore every petal: I hope that one day we can finally call you a man because even little boys understand a woman's command and the meaning of the simplest words like "no" seem to escape you. You taught me that instead I am a tree, strong, timeless, as the leaves will always come back even after the harshest of winters and to stay away from flower pickers.

To the boy who wrapped up my cuts and healed my heart with every bandaid and strip of gauze: I hope you never lose your sense of compassion in an unforgiving world. You taught me that laughter really is the best medicine and now I laugh in even the most awkward of situations.

To the man who stole my mother's attention and broke her spirit: I hope your loneliness will fade because why else would you pick a fight right when she wanted to go if not for her to stay on the phone, driving for hours, screaming at you because she needed the last word. You taught me that people do horrible things to not be alone and gave me car sickness.

To my father whose mindset is stuck in war torn Lebanon and thinks he needs to protect me from reality: I hope you embrace the modern world one day and realize having pride does not equate to a fragile ego. You forced taught me to burst the bubble you created and how to live life outside of your my comfort zone.

To my baby brother who I never thought I would want and realized that I most certainly needed: I hoped you would never feel the pains of growing up but because that's unrealistic, I wept the first time I held you. You taught me pure, unadulterated joy is real.

To the boy who loved me with small actions and big words: I hope you find someone who will encourage your filmmaking because, like they say, the silver screen is forever and your only problem was that you believed in infinities. You taught me that art is living; it is the artist's burden to capture it, and I was the most delightful challenging muse.

And,

To the men reading this essay who have a hand in deciding my path: I hope you don't mind that I am older than my years. Our age should be measured in experiences and moments instead of years because some people live more in 5 years than others do in 50. If we're following this measure of age, than I am 36 years old, not 17, and this is all thanks to the men who come and go in the revolving door that is my life.

Sincerely,
the rambler

Takeaways

Write what you want to write, however you want to write it.

Why this essay?

Context. Stanford wants to understand the context that surrounds you, the cultural milieu in which you were formed. The personal essay is a chance for them to get to know you, on a visceral level. This applicant took the opportunity to share what she thought was most important to her; little bits and pieces of her life which made her who she is today, pieces that certainly couldn't be expressed in a dreary activities list or additional information box. Unfortunately, the applicant didn't tie this essay in with the rest of her application—a flaw that the admissions committee specifically noted.

How was this essay written?

The structure of this essay—as a series of parting notes to the men in this applicant's life, is unique and powerful. These little vignettes are windows into the severe adversity that this applicant faced, alternating between positive and negative experiences.

The last paragraph directly addresses the admissions officer (who, incidentally, was female). It's a great twist to a remarkable essay.

What Stanford said

"PE: Very strong PE, shows immense character and strength"
"PE: after reading [NAME]'s PE, it is unfortunate to see that the only mention of the humanities within her major interests is CS + Writing. "

Concluding remarks

This is an essay that grabs you by the lapels and shakes you.

Sample III

As a kid, I would often venture out to the edge of the pond at the end of my street, where the cattails that poked out of the clear water grew thicker and taller until they towered over me into a grassy wetland that seemed to stretch on forever. Then, I would run and run, reeds snapping and crunching beneath my feet, until my house had disappeared completely from view, until the roar of the nearby highway faded into the rustling of tall grasses, until everything was unrecognizable except for the sky above my head. Immersed in the dense grasses, I would become a mischievous runaway, or a lost princess, or an intrepid explorer.

In play, I was shapeshifting, infinite. The prairie belonged to me. But according to the stories repeated all around me, the prairie belonged to the pioneers, heaving with dysentery as they crossed the plains in cramped covered wagons, braving bitter winds, killing turkeys, and fending off dangerous natives, so they could build log cabins and civilize the frontier. What belonged to me had been left behind long before I was born, when my parents immigrated from China. Here, I spoke 'surprisingly good English', was constantly asked for my 'real name' , and listened intently at school as we learned not only about the pioneers, but of a full cast of white men who had discovered the world. Then, we studied the Western canon in English and played European classical music in Orchestra. On my own time, I read books about mothers who called their daughters 'hon' and watched families say grace before dinner on television. I had no part in these stories. My classmates saw my black hair and almond eyes and deemed me shy and quiet (and good at math) before I even had the chance to open my mouth (or fail a calculus test). I found myself being talked over, pushed past in the halls. I stopped going out to the pond with the cattails.

At home, my parents told me stories about walking barefoot with their siblings to school, great-uncles escaping the Communists in the night, aunts working in re-education camps. I facetimed my grandma at night because she was on the other side of the world. We recited ancient poems about full moons and faraway homes. I debated my mother, argued with my sister, yelled about my hopes and dreams. But at school, surrounded by white classmates, I succumbed to the gap in the story. My every action boiled down to enforcing or defying a stereotype, and I strained to fit within this dichotomy. Despite the expansive grasslands we lived in, the limited narratives that existed for Asian people did not grant me enough space to be a full person.

Still, when I thought of home, alongside memories of folding over-stuffed dumplings with my family and speaking broken Mandarin, I always remembered the bluestems in the park brushing against my calves, smelled the ash of controlled burns in the fall, felt the soft black soil of my backyard between my toes. I wondered: What if I been told a different story about the prairie?

I began to seek out stories that could expand this limited narrative. I read novels written by people of color. I wrote poems and made art that explored the nuances of my experience. I was able to take a course in which I learned American history through the discussion of multiple perspectives. I joined a club that helped me start conversations with students and faculty about race and inequity. Gradually, I carved out new space that included my voice. Then, I began to reclaim my home. I took long sunset runs through local restorations, planted milkweed with my friends, hiked grassland trails, and knew that no matter what I was told, I was an integral part of this place, and it was an integral part of me.

Takeaways

Zoom out, and then back in.

Why this essay?

The writer fleshes out the motivation, and personal backstory, behind her interest in identity and sociology. This complements her stellar list of activities centered around cultural engagement and activism, and creates a narrative of someone deeply engaged with questions of social identity.

How was this essay written?

This applicant has exceptional command of prose, and an amazing ability to guide the reader along a seamless stream of ideas. She uses this to good effect—starting with a

Her struggles with her own identity and cultural "fit" are introduced with a series of vivid specific examples, countenanced by humor ("failed a calculus test").

What Stanford said

"PE shows keen social awareness, SE shows excitement for learning which is appealing

PE: dealing w/ racial stereotypes, sought out different narratives to carve out a space of belonging"

Concluding remarks

An exceptionally written essay that imparts a clear picture of the applicant.

Sample IV

Some might say it's emasculating to have a butterfly as a spirit animal. Perhaps I should've gone with the dragon—my Chinese nickname—but the resourceful Viceroy butterfly Limenitis archippus created an identity too relatable to pass up.

I was tricked into learning the viola in 6th grade. The orchestra director distributed lychee jellies to all orchestra students during morning practice sessions. At first, I resisted the temptation, but once she offered mango drops, I caved like Persephone eating the pomegranates. Hades would've been proud; Mrs. McClellan invited me to the viola section (affectionately called music's Underworld) with the enticing nectar, and I, like Persephone, migrated eagerly.

The Underworld turned over a new leaf for the caterpillar to chew on. Complex chord structures. Fast-paced vibratos. Beautiful, drawn-out trills and tensioned octaves overlapping with grace notes. In music, I realized my power to hover between the different flowers of musical styles. Wagner's graceful lulls intertwined with Strauss's angst to create layers for hiding under—worlds of raw emotion and elegance concealed by camouflage; the world I desired to enter the most was the All-State Orchestra.

I didn't make All-State the first year I auditioned, but the emotional bond between music and me compelled me to continue. The system favored the Monarch caterpillars—wealthy children with European instruments, private instructors, and tiger parents who pushed them into practicing. However, I was just a Viceroy caterpillar unable to afford all of those privileges.

My rejection motivated me to broaden my instrument range. Each of my instruments embodies a part of my personality. Stella, my introverted viola, whispers lullabies, but she sometimes lacks the confidence of the European violas because she suspects that she was cheaper. I rescued Draco the Bass from the storage closet (named for my zodiac and envy of Harry Potter). He had obviously been working part-time shifts after school; although his pegs are worn and he has tic-tac-toe tattoos engraved in his wood, his sarcastic persona sometimes slips a witty tease. Adeline the Piano, named after "Ballade pour Adeline," the first song I practiced improvising on, shares my guilty pleasure of reading rom-com novels. Nicholas the Guitar, although raised Christian, questions society's mandates. He's empathetic and often feels the need to remind me that the Earth and I are not the center of the solar system. Between the five of us, we fluttered between swing jazz, waltzy adagios, and modern pop; our unique voices blended to create musical covers and original compositions. And through this instrumental phase of metamorphosis, I progressed from my caterpillar stage to a chrysalis.

Like the harmless Viceroy butterfly utilizing batesian mimicry and adopting the coloration of the toxic Monarch butterfly, I—through YouTube—copied the idiosyncrasies of the world's best string players. By incessantly pausing and resuming clips, I perceived the slight adjustments these Monarchs made. Bozo Paradzik favors a stiff left hand and a German bow to force pressure, Rinat Ibragimov tilts the angle of his bowings to slide quick crescendos, and [NAME] drifts through hundreds of their videos. I sorted through dozens of camera angles and hours of tutorials to substitute for the world I wasn't allowed to enter because of cost barriers. Although I envied the pace of metamorphosis of the privileged Monarch pupae, I trusted my mimicry to hold its own.

During the second audition year, I dragged both Stella and Draco to the All-State warm-up room. Draco was up first, and he timidly crawled into the audition room, his frame slouched forward and endpin scraping across the floor.

"Sight-reading excerpt two."

A lyrical piece. Just focus on mixing Rabbath's vibrato with Robinson's tone.

The fourth line of the excerpt climaxed at a high E flat. Fourth position. A difficult pitch to nail, but we've sung this before.

I fluttered through the chromatic scale to reach the note, vibrato-ing the E flat.

Holding the note for ... One.

Two.

Three.

And I sneezed.

I paused, momentarily distracted.

I did what I should've done the second I left my cocoon.

I raised my wings

And I flew.

... Two acceptances and Principal Chair Bassist.

Takeaways

Find the extraordinary in the ordinary.

Why this essay?

It's clear that this student has a passion for music—for all sorts of genres and instruments. He shares this passion at both a high level, in metaphor, and at a low level, through short vignettes describing the personalities of his instruments. But the deeper purpose of this essay is to help the reader understand his personality, and outlook on the world. The tone of the essay is informal, honest, and down-to-earth; a quality that is difficult to get right, and something the admissions officers specifically commented on.

How was this essay written?

It's a tricky thing to distinguish an essay about All-State from the legions of other essays on the same topic. This writer takes an unconventional tact, using All-State as a specific example of how his musical pursuits have helped him grow.

There's plenty of great prose to take note of in this essay.

The metaphor of the Viceroy butterfly is elegant and powerful, serving as a seamless way to disarm common presumptions *"Monarch caterpillars—wealthy children with European instruments, private instructors, and tiger parents"* and introduce his final acceptance into All-State as *"I raised my wings. And I flew."* The personification of his instruments is a vivid way to showcase the time and effort—the dedication and familiarity—the applicant has with his craft.

What Stanford said

"nice PE about music. no significant evidence of depth of thought or noncogs. Sincere, light, open. Humility evident. An introspective, realistic writer."

Concluding remarks

A great spin on a lifelong passion.

Sample V

Few tasks are as intimidating as parallel parking, but for me, this challenge seemed more like a relevant metaphor. For as long as I can remember, my mother would commit to a parking spot and remain steadfast—no matter the constraints. "I swear I can make it," she insisted. However, my mother neglected to consider the vast array of other options, and fell into a convergent mindset.

One time, in particular, is ingrained into my memory. Weekly, my mother and I went to the Farmers' Market. Eyeing a "rock-star parking spot," she haphazardly turned on her blinkers and initiated the park.

"WHAT ARE YOU DOING?" I screamed as cars whizzed past us on the bustling avenue downtown, shaking the Toyota Highlander with the gusts of wind.

"How could we pass up this spot?" she followed up, as if she were naive enough to ignore the surrounding hoards of traffic.

"There are plenty of other spots!" I remarked.

"This spot has our names on it!" she exclaimed.

Therein lies the metaphor: parallel parking means fitting into an enclosed space, just as one tries to fit into and identify with a place in society. The hallmark The Breakfast Club quote struck me as eerily relevant: "You see us as you want to see us—in the simplest of terms, in the most convenient definitions." Even from a young age, I struggled to identify with superlatives that my peers fell into so easily. They were quick to deem themselves as "athletes," "artists," or "academics." In truth, I was all of those things, yet I never conformed; I couldn't seem to locate my single "parking place" in life.

My town championed a conservative approach to personal expression. Classmates ostracized me for only socializing with my female counterparts; fellow swimmers hid my keys after officially coming out in junior year. I soon realized that I would have to deal with small-town closed-mindedness due to my identity.

However, things began falling into place after I immersed myself in the RYLA, when I was chosen to be a team counselor to guide other high school leaders in reaching an enlightened understanding of themselves. The most quintessential component of the conference involves counselor testimonials, where counselors pour out their life stories to expose their vulnerabilities, along with the lessons learned along their journeys. On July 17, I found myself staring into a crowd of three hundred strangers. I felt the same rush of adrenaline and fear fill my head as I flashed back to the frightening experience of my mother's arbitrary parking scene.

I finally built up the courage to unapologetically say, "I'm gay," in front of people I'd never met before. I was showered with hugs and support from people I'd never met before—something I'd never experienced before. I had been so used to the judgment and shunning after I told people my secret, that I'd been completely desensitized to acceptance. It struck me—there's a bigger world outside of small-town Iowa.

Though growing up in rural Iowa posed significant struggles, it made me the person I am today—full of grit and perseverance. Since rejecting conformity, I unapologetically live in my own terms. I am proud of my diverse background and interests; they make me who I am and reaffirm the values I uphold.

Realizing that upholding identities that deviated from society's norm was not something to fear, I choose to share my story, rather than fear it. Similar to my brief run-in with death, I still feel equivalent emotions whenever I become vulnerable about my background. However, the impact I can have on others is immeasurable.

Takeaways

Identity can be defining, but not totalizing.

Why this essay?

This essay describes the student's identity through the clever metaphor of *parallel parking*. By talking about his sexual orientation in the personal essay, the student has a chance to share an integral part of his identity that might otherwise be difficult to incorporate elsewhere in his application. After reading this essay, the reader peeks into the unique experiences and struggles that molded the student, as well as his perseverance in embracing an identity that his community shunned.

How was this essay written?

Parallel parking—and crazy parents, for that matter—is an experience to which everyone can relate, yet unique enough to be memorable (after all, the admissions officer commented "metaphor of parallel parking, quirky but it works"). Finally—this student didn't play identity politics; instead, they waited until the 8th paragraph to talk about his sexual orientation, and focused on how it influenced his growth, all while subtly highlighting his high school activities.

What Stanford said

"PE: owning identity, politically active in a conservative community, metaphor of parallel parking, quirky but it works"

Concluding remarks

All in all, an effective essay.

Intellectual Vitality

The Stanford community is deeply curious and driven to learn in and out of the classroom. Reflect on an idea or experience that makes you genuinely excited about learning.

The What

As one of the most notorious essays on Stanford's application, the intellectual vitality essay has troubled just about every applicant we've heard from. To admissions officers, it doesn't matter if you took fifteen AP exams if it was your parents who pushed you to do so—they want to know that you have a genuine love for learning.

What separates two applicants with identical test scores? Chances are, one of them can demonstrate a stronger commitment to learning. In 250 words, tell Stanford what it is that makes you want to learn.

The Why

Stanford wants its campus to be an oasis of lively academic discourse, which is why admissions officers look for students who can share and develop new ideas. In fact, Stanford values intellectual vitality so much that admissions officers' work cards have a dedicated sections for comments about this particular essay.

The Pitfalls

Be creative, but genuine. In particular:

Don't be boring. If you love physics, the best way to show that probably isn't talking about self-studying for the AP Physics exam. Instead, consider talking about an experience that made you interested in physics in the first place.

Don't lie. It's easy to tell you're making something up when you throw in names of authors you haven't read or discuss a subject you clearly don't know enough about.

Don't be superficial. Though you're only asked to discuss an event or experience that made you interested in learning, be sure to write more than just that. Consider writing about how that experience has shaped your academic interests today.

The How

Take a step back. What makes you curious? What makes you lost in your thoughts? Is there a topic that you can talk to someone for *hours* about?

This is one of the tougher essays to write—please, don't try to crank it out in one sitting. While it's good to talk about something captivating over something mundane, anything has the potential to work here. Most importantly, keep in mind that admissions officers just want to know that there's more to you than just doing homework and going out.

Sample I

I was 13 and bored, looking for something to watch on Netflix. On a whim, I chose *Doctor Who*, a show recommended to me by my dad. The British accents were a bit off-putting, the special effects comical, but I was blown away. I could feel the couch under my legs and the blanket clutched in my hands, but all I could see was the Doctor and his adventures. He was so clever, able to defeat his enemies with a plan, not a weapon; he was funny, able to reassure people in times of crisis; most outstanding to me, he was full of wonder and a sense of adventure. The Doctor managed to put into words a feeling I have known my whole life: There is so, so much to see.

The world is full of books to be read and music to be enjoyed and people from all walks of life to meet. There are foods to taste and languages to learn and landmarks to take touristy pictures at. There are problems waiting to be solved, people in need of help, a lifetime of sunsets ready to be admired. You can never know everything, but there are so many options: airplanes? Computers? Electromagnetism? Psychology? Political science? I want as much knowledge as I can get.

If *Doctor Who* has taught me anything, it's to stop waiting and run. Run and see this wonderful world.

Takeaways

Lives to absorb the information around you.

Why this essay?

By writing this essay, the student concocts a unique way to tell her admissions officer that every subject is worth exploring and learning about.

How was this essay written?

This essay clearly shows that the student does not lock herself into one field of study; rather, she wants to learn about everything. The Doctor Who reference piques the reader's interest at the beginning and the last two sentences work together to pull the essay together nicely.

Concluding remarks

A light-hearted essay that gets the job done.

Sample II

When I was six years old, my mom took me to the local Barnes and Noble and let me buy any book I wanted. Being the typical six-year-old girl whose favorite color is pink, I ran over to the history section and picked up a pastel pink book, which happened to be a biography about Amelia Earhart.

After my mom bought me that biography, I rushed home and read through the book that same day. I was so intrigued by how Earhart was able to break gender barriers. Earhart made the six-year-old me realize that women can accomplish anything they put their heart into. I was so mesmerized by this story, I went back to the same section at Barnes and Noble and bought another book about the Revolutionary War. This happened every week for the next seven years. By then, I had amassed a collection with over 200 history books.

My friends think I'm "boring" for spending my weekends curled up in my bed reading a historical novel. But they don't understand the impact history has had on me. Ever since I bought that pink book, I have always been seeking to absorb more than I'm given. In history, whether it's a mistake or triumph, every event has a takeaway and has taught me lessons I wouldn't have learned anywhere else. From watching a documentary on the Civil War to actually visiting a battle site, everything about history excites me and inspires me to continue to learn more.

Takeaways

The pursuit of knowledge can be all-consuming, in a beautiful way.

Why this essay?

Collecting over two hundred history books is quite impressive. Not only is this essay a unique way to show the writer's love for history, it also shows how an experience as mundane as going to the bookstore can turn lead to a passion for learning.

How was this essay written?

Candid and well-paced, this essay leaves out many of the ornate bells-and-whistles we see in other essays and still manages to convey a strong message. Indeed, the plainness of her writing style works in her favor and establishes this essay as an honest, straightforward discussion of her interest in history.

Concluding remarks

A coherent essay that clearly shows the writer's passion in history.

Sample III

"Excuse me, do you have any ziploc bags that I could borrow?" I asked the withered coding professor at GHP as I popped into his room at nine P.M., "It's an emergency, and I just saw the biggest boll weevil and I need it for my neuroscience project." Startled, the professor pulled out a most sophisticated tool of capture: a red Solo cup. He handed me the cup, much to the bewilderment of my music major friend who muttered something along the lines of "crazy science majors" as I started spewing facts about the weevil's impressive track record of destroying cotton and its extensive migrational patterns. Unabashed, I scooped up the weevil and placed it within the terrarium that my instructor had lent me.

I first encountered the boll weevil and its other evil associates in the Science Olympiad event Invasive Species. It was one of the events overshadowed by big name events such as Anatomy and Physiology and Thermodynamics, but it was an event that was wholly mine. I put dozens of hours into my thick, three-ringed binder because I loved exploring the disruption of environment that these organisms caused. Joining this event has fostered a love for conservation, and I eventually branched out to compete in other earth science events such as Hydrogeology, Ecology, Dynamic Planet, and Herpetology. Science Olympiad has made me realize that learning should not be limited to grades; learning encompasses passion and curiosity buried within an ingrained desire to explore the world.

Takeaways

Learning should be an integral part of life.

Why this essay?

With this essay, the writer reveals a deep passion for the sciences that complements the rest of his science-oriented application.

How was this essay written?

The writer's excitement over a boll weevil is a humorous introduction that leads nicely into his passion for science. By referring to the Invasive Species event as "wholly mine," he demonstrates a strong interest in the sciences that he laters reinforces by listing other science events he has eventually competed in.

Concluding remarks

Another example of a straightforward essay that conveys the writer's desire to learn more.

Sample IV

I traveled to Rwanda to learn how to forgive. While studying the genocide in school, I was told the country overcame because of forgiveness. But how was forgiveness possible?

Months later, I was in Rwanda, hoping to have my questions answered. With my feet sinking into the mud, I battled the language barrier to ask a convicted perpetrator, "Why did you do it?"

He broke eye contact.

"We had a bad government."

I was unconvinced, and my questions remained unanswered. I conversed with Carl Wilkens, a missionary and the only American to stay during the genocide, questioning the idea that "everything happens for a reason." I was aghast at how other countries perpetuated the tragedy. A journalist told us the least Clinton could have done was acknowledge the genocide—even that would have made a difference.

But I also felt inspired. From watching the first all-women's drumming group to finding beauty in a memorial at a former killing site, Rwanda was breathtaking. Piles of tattered clothes resembled the hilly landscape, and light shining through shrapnel holes evoked the star-filled night sky. This juxtaposition was something I could not experience in a classroom.

In Rwanda, I learned it is possible to come back from anything. More broadly, I witnessed the value of immersive education. History cannot be fully grasped through textbooks—it is best understood by hearing others' stories in person. As a political science major, these experiences are crucial to my education. By embracing discomfort, we learn from those we disagree with.

Takeaways

Firsthand experiences are crucial to understanding the world.

Why this essay?

Difficult topics require intellectual maturity, and the writer proves in this essay that she is ready to deal with those topics. In fact, she already has.

How was this essay written?

Seamlessly blending a unique trip to Rwanda with her desire to learn about the world, the writer crafts a serious narrative that responds to the prompt. One of her admissions officers praised the "depth" of this essay, and we would agree.

Concluding remarks

An effective essay that shows the writer's willingness to engage in difficult discussions.

Sample V

Sitting in my freshman Honors Biology class, notebook and highlighters neatly organized on my lab table—this is where I fell in love. No, not with a person, but a carcinogenic concept. It may be alarming for some to think about it, a fifteen-year-old girl infatuated with oncology; however, it was an inspiration for me. At this very point in my life, I began to know why I was working so hard in school, why I wanted so desperately to help others. Just the idea of studying, diving deeper into such a field excited me to no end. I could not wait to specialize in this medical profession, anxiously awaiting graduation and college even though I had not yet begun to experience high school. Well, that is until it happened.

At the end of my freshman year, I found out my grandfather had a brain tumor. His death shattered me, and the fact that those little malignant cells were the cause just irked me. If I did not want to change the future of medicine more before, I definitely did now. I never wanted anyone else to experience the pain and loss I felt, the one my best friend felt when her dad passed away from prostate cancer, like what any victim of cancer's family felt. No, I wanted and still want families to celebrate and cry tears of joy when their loved one survives, is cured and cancer free. I want to change the face of cancer research and treatment.

Takeaways

Personal tragedies can serve as motivation for noble causes.

Why this essay?

The writer frames the grim passing of her grandfather in a strong narrative about her desire to help improve the world through oncology. She is terse but her words carry weight—one admissions officer simply commented, "Well done."

How was this essay written?

A plain but well-structured essay about her passion for medicine. Everything in this essay is organized and balanced appropriately. The reader can fully understand and appreciate her immense drive to learn.

Concluding remarks

A mature essay that provides solid backgrounding for the writer's academic interests.

Roommate Letter

Virtually all of Stanford's undergraduates live on campus. Write a note to your future roommate that reveals something about you or that will help your roommate—and us—get to know you better.

The What

Write a letter to your future roommate.

A literal letter. Friendly. Informal. Not an essay. Think of this as a letter you'd write to a friend. One catch—their mom reads it first. Maybe you like leaving dirty socks around the room, to soak up all the beer you spill. Maybe that's chill with your roommate. It's probably not chill with their mom. This letter is a first date; you won't be able to reveal all the glorious complexities and intricacies of who you are, but you'll hopefully be able to use a shallow characterization of yourself to leave a good impression.

After the first month on campus, my hall read our roommate essays to eachother—what a lark.

The Why

At this point, the reader is (hopefully) thinking, "I totally get it—this applicant is going to be one of the next big movers and shakers. The next Einstein, Elvis, Eisenhower. But what, exactly, is this person like?" Your recommendation letters and interview notes give a shallow view of your personality—this essay is a way to let the admissions officer know things that you left out while chatting with some alumnus in a contrived coffeeshop conversation.

The Pitfalls

The best thing you can do is make the reader feel like you'd belong on campus. We don't really have a specific "cultural fit" outside of vague West Coast vibes, so readers are looking mostly for interesting kids, who are ready to get involved, be social, and be someone they'd like to meet.

The worst thing you can do is be unlikeable. Mean. Weird. Awkward. If your roommate reads your letter, and wants to move out, that's a bad sign. So, please, test it out (with adult readers, not kids). Ask folks how they would describe the person they met in the roommate letter, and see if it lines up with what you wanted to portray. Ask if they'd let their kid live with this person.

The How

This is an essay with a lighter tone, balancing out heavier questions like the "What is meaningful" question. We're asking about you; we want to know about you. So ... Tell them who you are. Tell them what you're like. Tell them what you're excited about! What you're looking forward to. Crack a lame joke. After all, you'll be spending at least a year, if not a lifetime, together.

Sample I

I like working with my hands and running through the woods. I keep my nails short so I can dig into my cello fingerboard, and avoid letting charcoal, clay, and other art/life detritus to gather underneath them and turn my cuticles into hideous swamp monster claws. A vocational survey once recommended I become the driver of a cement mixing truck, but I'm not sure Stanford offers that major. I touch lots of dirt (I'm bringing plants!) and give lots of hugs because they both increase serotonin levels in the brain. Speaking of hugs, if you need me, I'll be there for you. I like to think I give sound advice, and I will never leave you on read.

I promise I'll fight the urge to scribble all over our dorm walls. I'm an artist, and also an anarchist. I regularly fight the Man by cutting bagels into chunks instead of slicing them through the middle, putting the 'R' earbud into my left ear, and refusing to limit my perception of other people by the trappings of their identity. These are vital, but they are never your sole distinguishing features. I will strive to understand you as the full, multitudinous person you are.

I'm excited to meet you! When making art, I start with nothing and simply trust in my ability to make something beautiful. I take the same approach to making friends. So even though I don't know you yet, I trust that we will have a great time together.

Analysis

This is an excellent roommate essay. The second paragraph is an excellent highlight on the applicant's strong background in civil activism, while still being down-to-earth. There's plenty of good gag lines: "I become the driver of a cement mixing truck," and "I regularly fight the Man by cutting bagels into chunks." Reading this, you can tell exactly what kind of person the writer is, what they're interested in, and how sociable and engaged they are.

Sample II

People are like matryoshka dolls: on the inside, there's a whole other person.

On the outside, I love being alive. I love the world and being in it. I want to see and learn everything. I want to meet all the interesting people in the world, visit all the cool places, learn every language, and experience the full gamut of emotions available to humans. I want to go to the Moon and see the Earth from above, I want to learn the fundamental laws of nature, and find out why everything exists in the first place. I want the full experience.

But on the inside, sometimes, I am empty. I isolate myself, drowning in a pool of emotions and self-destruction. On the inside, I'm just trying to get through the day. There are scars on my skin, more than I can count, from moments when I was absolutely, completely hopeless.

Future Roommate, know this: sometimes I am quiet. Sometimes I just stop in the middle of a laugh. You'll ask, "you okay?" I'll reply, "just tired." Know this: I need distractions. I need hope. I need shelter from reality. I need to not feel numb. I'll listen to happy music and talk to those who love me and I'll feel better.

My two selves coexist. For years, I felt like falling apart. Now, I see my scars, I look up to the stars, and I know that somehow, impossibly, in spite of all my hopeless moments—I am okay.

Analysis

This is not a standard roommate essay. In fact, it's risky. The applicant bares their insecurities around loneliness and depression—showing a degree of self-awareness. They felt that this was an important element of their application, and chose to showcase it in this medium.

It certainly made the readers take note—they rarely comment on roommate essays, but both readers commented on this one, writing:

"RM: expresses inner isolation and occasional emptiness (DOFT check)"

"RM: struggles w/ isolation noted"

Sample III

Hey roommate,

How are you? Are you excited? Nervous? I know I am. I recently watched a movie about a psychotic girl who tries to kill her college roommate. I guess that doesn't exactly set the best precedent as far as college roommates go. But I assure, I, in no way, resemble that girl. So, I just wanted to tell you a few things about myself to put your mind at ease. I go to boarding school so I've lived in dorms all my life. I watch a lot of horror movies even though they give me nightmares. I like plants, although I'm not very good with them. I come with a supply of ramen noodles because let's be honest, ramen is delicious. On the subject of food, I would like to mention that Tibetan food is fantastic. And if you haven't tried it, we'll rectify that situation immediately. I'm an excellent sleeper, so don't worry about have having the lights on or working late. I have terrible vision in one eye so I wear glasses. Sometimes when I forget, I turn my head one way and squint. It's slightly creepy to be on the receiving end of this look (I've been told), but I'm just trying to focus. One last thing- my current roommate said her favorite thing about me was my habit of folding clothes when I'm stressed. So if you're closet is unorganized, you're in luck.

I'm so excited to see you!

[NAME]

Analysis

This essay is pretty funny—starting off directly with "I recently watched a movie about a psychotic girl who tries to kill her college roommate." It's also refreshingly direct and honest, with great quotes like "It's slightly creepy to be on the receiving end of this look". If you feel the tone of the rest of your application is a bit too formal, the roommate essay is a perfect place to balance that out.

Sample IV

Dear future roommate,

My name is [NAME], but you can call me [NICKNAME]. Here are some things you should know about me:

I think in puns and occasionally speak in hashtags. I'm fluent in four languages: English, Spanish, Spanglish, and meme. You'll likely hear these when I'm on the phone with my parents, who immigrated to California from Colombia but never left their culture behind.

I like to say that I'm a product of science because I was conceived in a petri dish. I attribute my ability to lick my elbow and other superhuman powers to this. But at 12 years old, I was disappointed to discover that I was not, in fact, a demigod. Still, while I may not be the daughter of Poseidon, nothing makes me feel more alive than swimming in the icy Northern California waves. Maybe we can take up surfing together.

I'm definitely a night person—expect to hear my philosophical questions, ethical dilemmas, and startup ideas around 2 am. But there are a few things I'll get up early for, such as kickboxing (the best way to de-stress) and the unparalleled sunrise from Mount Tam. I like to start my mornings by listening to podcasts, drinking yerba mate, and recounting my latest dream.

But enough about me—I want to know about you. What do you love? What would you fight for? Why do you see the world the way you do? We'll have so much to learn from each other.

Your future friend,

[NAME]

Analysis

Again, note the highlighting of other meaningful elements of the writer's background in a subtle, funny, fashion—from her immigrant heritage "I'm fluent in four languages: English, Spanish, Spanglish, and meme," to her IVF "I was conceived in a petri dish. I attribute my ability to lick my elbow and other superhuman powers to this." This essay gives a strong impression of a likeable individual who's ready to seize the day.

Sample V

If you ask me, the most beautiful place in the world is Tanzania. One of our two amusement parks is a safety hazard. Our electricity is a joke. And if you thought you have come across slow internet, think again. But Tanzania is still the most beautiful place to me. It's the people. The people here are always smiling, they are welcoming and trusting. They are warm. So, Hello future roommate! My name is [NAME] and I'm from Tanzania. I smile often. I like to think that I'm warm and welcoming. I'm certain that I'm both very trusting and trustworthy. And I am excited to meet you. I'm very much a comedy type of girl—*How I Met Your Mother*, *That 70s Show*, *The Simpsons*, and *Brooklyn Nine-nine*, are my all-time favorite shows. I sleep like a log at night, so nothing you could do can wake me up. Apparently, I have an awful taste in music. In my defense, it's not a crime to like a little bit of everything. Rest assured that whatever you like to listen to, I will too. I'll most certainly come across as shy at first, but within a few hours, I'll be cracking you up with my many expressive repetitive stories. I don't mind any question you could have about Africa or Tanzania. I hope you won't mind my questions—I've always loved learning about other people and places. And, I truly can't wait to make Stanford our home together.

Analysis

This essay is more direct, stating outright: "I'm warm and welcoming.", "I'm both very trusting and trustworthy," and "I've always loved learning about other people and places." And yet, the way these statements are written make them the natural implication of the flow of the essay. The applicant has elected to place heavy emphasis on her own background and origins, but shows how they also love engaging with the cultural hodgepodge of the Western world.

What is Meaningful

Tell us about something that is meaningful to you, and why?

The What

We all have something in our lives that we care about. It could be the stories your grandmother told you as a child, or it could be your dedication towards social equality. Find something that's meaningful to you, and tell Stanford about it.

Admissions officers are not here to judge, so be brave and choose a topic that you think you're best suited to writing about. Show them that you live for a reason.

The Why

Admissions officers want to see that you think for yourself, and you're not just a mindless zombie roaming around taking AP classes because your parents tell you to. Whatever is meaningful to you shines a light on the way you think and the way you act, and admission officers are interested in seeing if you really are the smart, well-adjusted individual your test scores and extracurricular activities make you out to be.

The Pitfalls

Common topics include family and friends, and it doesn't mean you shouldn't write about those. But do make sure that you're creative when it comes to the *why?* part. It's all too easy to make this essay overly formulaic, and your goal is to do the exact opposite.

The How

Aside from being an opportunity to demonstrate unique thinking, this essay is also a great place to showcase your writing skill. Try to craft a compelling narrative that helps tie the rest of your application together. If you're a STEM student, consider using this space to break out of the cold, formal-reasoning stereotype and show the admission officers your softer, more thoughtful side.

Sample I

Among the clutter of books, stray papers, candles and fake plants on my desk is a single glass jar of soil. It's not really the most aesthetically pleasing of decor, but it serves a symbolic purpose. Over time it's become one of my most valuable possessions. A friend's mother went to Lhasa, Tibet on vacation recently and asked me if I wanted her to bring anything back. I said I wanted some soil. She gave me a slightly quizzical look, but agreed anyway. She understood what soil from Tibet would mean to me. I know, it's incredibly cheesy, but it's the closest I will realistically ever get to home. I wanted something I could physically see everyday to remind myself of where I come from, and where I hope to return one day. I decided that if I couldn't travel to Tibet myself, I could at least have a piece of my home on my desk. My experiences of Tibet come entirely from the stories I was told by my father and my older relatives. I think it is common among second generation Tibetan refugees to feel slightly nostalgic for a country most of us haven't experienced. Despite the fact that I've never experienced Tibet first hand, I always imagine the possibility of going to Tibet as a grand return, of going home. The soil reminds me I am never too far away from that dream.

Why this essay?

Identity is often the most important part of a person, and it can give insight into an applicant's personal context. Because Stanford values diversity in its admissions, it's often a good idea to describe your background and personal identity somewhere in your application.

How was this essay written?

Poetic and sentimental with a strong command of language, this essay is an elegant reflection of the writer's unique personal identity. The jar of Tibetan soil on her desk, a powerful metaphor for her heritage, holds the essay together very nicely and leaves the reader satisfied.

Concluding remarks

A charming essay that describes the writer's background.

Sample II

In first grade, I wrote my first ever school paper: "How to Make Wine." Unsurprisingly, my parents received a phone call from my perplexed teacher. Unbeknownst to her, "making wine" was part of my life, having grown up helping my parents in our family vineyard.

Each summer, I've spent weeks working diligently in the vineyard with my family, pulling leaves, tucking branches, and trying to keep the vines healthy. Fall arrives, and our friends and family come to help harvest. Like clockwork, the cycle continues each year. The days blur together in an endless stream of routine—pull, prune, pick, repeat. However, we remain focused and persevere, knowing the crop will prosper under our care.

The grapes are an extension of our family—we tend them, and they reward us accordingly. Doing things the proper way (even though it may take longer) gives tangible results, like the sweet juice which trickles from the press after a long day of harvesting.

I've grown up with those vines. My parents' ideology, of putting in the extra time and effort into a task, has been subtly instilled into my being. Whether I'm working on a problem set with friends, or collaborating on a research project, I advocate that we take the extra time to understand the process and work together. Unconsciously, the vineyard, my home, has taken seed in my soul, helping to shape me just as I have helped shape it.

Why this essay?

There's really no set format for this essay, and you can choose to write about virtually anything. In this case, the writer discusses the importance of putting in time and work to reap the sweet fruits of her labor. Instead of directly telling admissions officers about her well-adjusted personality, this writer clever wraps everything up in a story about her upbringing.

How was this essay written?

The essay begins with a humorous anecdote about winemaking with her family, and gradually extends her family tradition into a metaphor about focus, patience, and perseverance. By sticking to plain and candid language, she shows that her positive attitude is simply a part of her identity.

Concluding remarks

A polished essay that gives nice insights into the writer's demeanor and approach toward what she does.

Sample III

"Your rook is mine!" I exclaimed with glee, moving my own queen to capture my father's apparently exposed piece.

"Really?" my dad replied as he deftly moved a bishop back to capture my queen.

Groaning at the short-lived nature of my victory, my dad smiled. "You'd do well to remember that not much is truly yours." As a seven-year-old whose primary strategy was to trade evenly, I marveled at the relative depth of my father's strategy. Remembering his words, I managed to beat him a few weeks later. I haven't won since, but I still haven't forgotten his words.

"Not much is truly yours."

When my parents threatened to take away my favorite toys if I didn't eat my vegetables, I learned that my possessions were not always mine.

When I crashed my bike and flew off the handlebars, sustaining a nauseating blow to my head, I learned my body was not always mine.

When I flipped through my digital camera's old photos and see my little brother as a baby, now seven, I learned that time was not always mine.

But, when I confessed to stealing a pack of gum from the store, when I tried remaining calm instead of shouting at my parents, when I tried to listen–not just hear–a friend's problem, I learned my mind is mine. Integrity. Rationality. Empathy. Ultimately, that afternoon chess game is meaningful because it taught me that my principles are the only things I can truly call my own.

Why this essay?

The message of the essay is that the applicant strongly values his principles. The applicant felt that the rest of the application painted a rosy picture of him as someone with strong academic achievements, but left out his personal motivation—a gap he addresses here.

How was this essay written?

The writer uses a sparse, story-telling style to show the reader how he thinks. Instead of writing in big paragraphs, sometimes it can be beneficial to do what this student does and break up your essay into smaller sections. However, this essay reads in a disorienting, unorganized manner—the first several paragraphs are sensationalist ways to restate a common idea, "Not much is mine," which has a loose tie to the message of the essay, which is "I have principles."

Concluding remarks

Balance being interesting with being convincing.

Sample IV

I've had Piggy since I was a baby. She's a little, pink stuffed baby cow with a decorative diaper, a snout that flaps, and curly ribbons on her head. Please don't think too deeply about her name; I really thought she was a pig. I couldn't sleep without her as a child, and she's accompanied me on all my family trips. We've trekked through jungles and crossed rivers in Ecuador, ridden in my grandmother's bicycle basket and strolled through the night market in Taiwan, and gotten lost on the streets of Japan together. Piggy's battle scars have long been sewn up by my mom, but they are still visible reminders of our journeys together. Piggy was my companion, and I've grown attached to her. She still sits on a shelf in my room, waiting for more love and adventure. Sometimes, I pick her up just to look at her, play with her curled ribbons the way I used to as a child, and recall the memories she represents. Now that I'm going off to new places to experience new things, I'll take Piggy along with me so that she doesn't miss a thing.

Why this essay

You can write your essay on just about anything—this writer chose to write about something as simple as a stuffed animal of hers. And yet, this essay demonstrates a much deeper theme: the writer's fondness of memories and experiences. Admissions officers are not looking for a specific thing here, but they want you to write about something that matters to you, and articulate it well.

How this essay was written

On the surface, this essay is just a simple laundry list of places the writer has been. But, if we look closer and read between the lines, we'll notice how she uses the story of her stuffed cow to show how much she treasures her experiences.

What Stanford said

"Stuffed cow triggers memories of journeys together"

Concluding remarks

Mundane is relatable.

Sample V

Every morning, my grandma would sit on a creaky folding chair on the stoop of my house and sip tea from a clunky thermos as she waited for the van that took her to the senior center. Sometimes, she would take naps from midday into the evening and still come out to wait when she woke up, no matter what time it was. Once, I came home late at night, and there she was, in the dark, clutching her thermos in the flimsy chair, quietly waiting for the van to come. In photo albums, she was a little girl hugging a stuffed rabbit, then a woman, laughing as she biked through the city, and then a grandmother, cradling my sister and me. But by the time I was old enough to wonder about the person in the photographs, she'd faded away under years of deafness and progressively worsening Alzheimer's. When she returned to live with us, we struggled to communicate with her, and she, likely over-whelmed by her rapidly decreasing personal agency, seemed to have given up. But my family hadn't: we began sitting down with her and writing her notes. I'd tell my mother something to ask her in broken Chinese. My mother would translate my message more smoothly, scrawl it onto a slip of paper, and show my grandmother, who would squint, read it, smile, and reply. As we patiently pushed through the barriers of language, hearing, and memory, my grandmother was able to tell her stories again.

Why this essay

Even in the face of seemingly every obstacle, this writer finds a way to express her love for family. Instead of letting "the barriers of language, hearing, and memory" stop her, she perseveres and lets her character and thoughtfulness shine through. Show admissions officers that you care.

How was this essay written

Powerful and effortlessly evocative, this essay paints a beautiful portrait of the writer's relationship with her grandmother. Through her exceptional choice of vocabulary and clear flow of ideas, the writer skillfully demonstrates what is most meaningful to her.

What Stanford said

"Heartwarming."

Concluding remarks

A wonderfully written essay that combines elements of family and heritage.

Short Essays

Significant Challenge

What is the most significant challenge that society faces today?

The What

What do *you* think is the most significant challenge the world faces? We're not asking you what *is* the biggest challenge out there, in the abstract. We're not asking you what challenge is the most well known, the most tractable, the most threatening, the most immediate. What do *you*, as an individual, consider the most significant challenge—the most important thing for you to work on? Guess what—there's a lot of important problems in the world. Absolutely none of them can be fully described in 50 words. Absolutely none of them can be worked on, solved, or even thought about, by everyone. Instead, people carry diverse perspectives, backgrounds, and experiences into their interactions with society. We find different problems because we search for different things.

The Why

Stanford wants you to demonstrate your passion. What's the niche Supreme Court opinion that only someone who's slogged through the courts would know? What's the social stigma that only someone who's been fighting at the front lines of reform would know? What's the medical condition that only someone who's been burning the midnight oil at the lab bench would know?

What sort of interesting problems have you run across, and what amazing things would happen once you've solved them?

The Pitfalls

The best thing you can do is flesh out your interests. The reader should finish your essay, and think one of two things: "Wow, I didn't know that before", or "Wow, I didn't think about it that way". They should read, and get a sense that you really know what you're talking about; what you've been working on.

The worst thing you can do is talk about a challenge that you don't care about, just because you think you have to. If you haven't done a whit of sustainability work, but you write about how global warming is *THE* existential threat, the admissions officer will be suspicious.

The How

This is a short essay, so jump right in. Short grabber—a stat or shocker. Elaborate. Hint at how you and what you've done fit in. Tell us the impact.

Sample I

The absence of communication is the challenge. A hate-torn nation stems from the pandemic disease of "us-versus-them". A simple concept to imagine: only "we" matter because "they" aren't "us". Don't you think it would be different if we didn't stop listening when we don't hear what we want to hear?

Sample II

Despite the growing importance of the internet in today's world, only about 14% of Africans are connected to the internet. From cloud services, connecting producers to their market, enhancing education, breaking communication barriers, and easier access to social services; connectivity to the internet is the solution Kenya, and Africa, needs.

Sample III

Empathy. Somehow, in an age where technology allows us to be so connected,we have become detached from each other. We maintain a terrifying level of apathy to situations that aren't directly relevant to ourselves. Encouraging dialogue that engages different people can help combat this illness.

Sample IV

This is GARBAGE. The paper, screen, or computer upon which this essay is read will inevitably become waste. This is THE challenge. It is imperative to develop an effective, global waste management system

… soon. Otherwise the byproducts of our human existence will surpass the Earth's capacity to absorb it.

Sample V

Immunotherapy, novel drugs, groundbreaking surgeries, and personalized therapies—all are now at the forefront of medicine. And yet, access is limited to those with means. Some of the most devastating diseases—cancer and infections—occur with greater frequency in developing nations. How can we increase access to life-saving treatments around the globe?

Last Two Summers

How did you spend your last two summers?

The What

This question is straightforward—what've you been up to in your last two summers? You've got to boil those 6 months down into 50 words.

The Why

Stanford wants to see two things: they want to see your intellectual vitality shine through, in how you've kept yourself busy outside of school. They want to see another side of you. They're wondering, rather than having an extra hour each day, what does the applicant do with an extra three months every year?

The Pitfalls

The best thing you can do is substantiate your story. Are you the Nobel Laureate in the making? Tell us about your research endeavours—your inventions or failures. Are you the next Super Bowl MVP? Tell us about your sports camps, or your practice regimen. If you're a writer, let them know what you wrote. If you're an activist, let us know how you acted. Take the chance to drive home your strongest activities or awards

… while keeping in mind you're human too; that you took the time to enjoy your break, that you went to the beach, read a book, met with friends.

The worst thing you can do is confuse the admissions officer. They want to see the depth of your commitment to things you've talked about in other parts of the application, not find out that you're secretly a pro poker player on the side. If you've been up to a lot of things—that's great! But do yourself a favor, and give your other pursuits more airtime than a one-liner in a 50 word essay. In particular, don't feel the need to list off 1000 things per summer, particularly if the last 998 weren't particularly meaningful or impactful. And trust me—you've been spending your summers in a meaningful way, even if you yourself don't think so.

The How

Most students just list—for good reason. Information density is high, and it gets straight to the point of the question. Paragraph or bullets—it really doesn't matter. If you're listing, put the most important thing in front, and let them know why it's important. Selective summer program? How selective? Research fellowship? What happened to the project? Summer camp? What'd you learn?

Another option is to expound on a single activity or experience. If you're expounding, have fun! Write informally, and like you're talking to a friend. Pick one or two things, and make the essay flow together in a cohesive whole.

Sample I

2017: AP Chemistry JHU CTY, Royal Palms Tennis Academy Camp, Quantum

Mechanics (EdX) Georgetown, Multivariable Calculus (MIT Open-CourseWare)

2018: Perimeter Institute ISSYP Program (4% Acceptance Rate), Chinese Bridge Summer

Program, Writing [NAME'S] Guide to AP Physics C: Mechanics and Electrodynamics Study Guides

Sample II

Learning Korean through a book borrowed from my Latin teacher, Latin-ing, hanging with Jen, trying to juggle (#3 on bucket list, you'll see later), praying, golfing, showing friends the wonders of Orange County's Little Saigon (Little Saigon is like a geode; it seems modest until you peek inside, please visit!)

Sample III

I attended nationals for dance in New York and Las Vegas, travelled the Rhone with my Grandma, interned with the Governor, saw Harry Styles in concert, reorganized my house, attended a Mercy Corps program, read and watched everything I couldn't during school, and had a few sunburns.

Sample IV

The methodical "click" of my pruning snips in the vineyard was intertwined with the snap of a micro-pipette tip disposal at lab. Weekends were filled with coffees, spontaneous dancing, and failed cooking attempts with friends. Relaxing and tanning (or burning) on the beach offered the perfect ending to my summers.

Sample V

I went outdoors whenever possible, created new friendships, strengthened old ones, spent time alone, volunteered at bilingual summer camps, performed Bach and Elgar, drove long distances, hung out with my grandma, searched for my artistic voice. I read widely and deeply. I found intrinsic motivation. I grew into myself.

Historical Moment

What historical moment or event do you wish you could have witnessed?

The What

Exactly as the prompt asks: if you could experience any historical moment or event, what would it be? You've probably taken a fair share of history classes by now. What historical events stand out to you? Is it Martin Luther King, Jr.'s "I Have a Dream" speech in Washington, D. C.? Or is it Robert E. Lee's surrender at Appomattox? Choose something that fascinates you.

The Why

You have to know the past to understand the present. Stanford wants to see what you're interested in. What motivates you. They're giving you an open ended prompt to give you a chance to expound on your interests, or showcase your awareness of the world around you.

The Pitfalls

It's always a good idea to make your application as coherent as possible, but that doesn't mean you should start Googling historical moments for ones that you think would fit best with your application. (Thousands of applicants probably have the same idea.)

The How

Don't sweat this essay—it won't make or break your application. Just pick a topic that interests you, and delve deep into its nuances. If it blends well with the rest of your application, even better!

Sample I

I wish I could have witnessed Hillary Clinton's inauguration. Our first female president would have continued the momentum of unprecedented change. I know it didn't really happen like the prompt suggests, but I wish I had. Girls everywhere would have grown up seeing that women can be successful anywhere.

Sample II

[NAME] and I stationed ourselves around the tree. We placed wire around all entrances, and each of us drank three cups of hot chocolate to sustain us for the night. Santa Claus was ours … but somehow we still fell asleep.

That crafty, old man eluded us that night. I want answers.

Sample III

I missed the era of astronauts and space shuttles. I would have been one of those obsessed kids who knows everything about each astronaut and all of their missions and clips all the newspaper articles. My mom watched the moon landing which BLOWS MY MIND.

Sample IV

At first I wanted to travel to the Roaring Twenties and to Jay Gatsby's mansion to experience the vibrant jazz and the upbeat tap-dancing—to observe firsthand the culture of conspicuous consumption and the Dadaism movement—but then I realized that I'm not white, and that would be a questionable journey.

Sample V

A petri dish of mold is sitting on the countertop—another failed experiment. And yet, instead of scrapping it, Alexander Fleming decided to investigate some of its properties, realizing the bacteria on the plate was dying. A simple mistake, but one that revolutionized the face of medicine as we know it.

Five Words

What five words best describe you?

Write 5 words. Easy as that. We're pretty sure the admissions officers don't really care about this question, as long as you don't do anything too strange. Please, please, don't be that kid that writes more than 5 words.

Here's a potpourri of examples:

Zealous, Tenacious, Versatile, Rationale, Committed

I only need one: underrated

avantgarde, imaginative, adaptive, pictorial, [NAME]

Spectacles, keyboard, questions, inventions, solutions

Renaissance (wo)man, proactive, empathetic, determined, human GPS

Driven, persistent, humorous, altruistic, inquisitive

Trustworthy, resilient, insightful, compelling, ambitious

spicy, conscientious, curious, involved, sister

Female reincarnation of Julius Caesar

Enthusiastic, curious, goofy, empathetic, awestruck

"What she wants, she earns"

Forward-looking, hustle-and-heart, link, sparkplug, loudspeaker

Determined, passionate, humorous, ambitious, hardworking

Empathetic, Skeptical, Pragmatic, Analytical, Ambitious

Determined, independent, optimistic, calm, outgoing

Sincere, Tenaciously Ambitious, Noteworthy Fortitude, Objectively Resilient, Developing ...

Spunky, Ambitious, Forthright, Charismatic, Bold

Inquisitive, Loquacious, Quirky, Driven, Persistent

Tenacious, creative, lively, caring, positive

irreverent, conscientious, creative, compassionate, in-progress

Activist, empathetic, networker, curious, adaptive

thankful, sponge, clumsy, playful, ready

Learn to lead by listening

Read, Listen, and Watch

When the choice is yours, what do you read, listen to, or watch?

This is another easy one. Just tell Stanford the types of books, movies, podcasts, and other media that you're interested in! Keep in mind that, although admissions officers are not looking for a correct answer here, but they do expect more than *Keeping Up With the Kardashians* and <insert trashy romance novel here>. Below are some examples:

I enjoy titles like *1984*, *The Good Earth*, and anything by Michael Crichton. For listening, I love The Great War, Tides of History, The 1975, and BORNS. When I have the remote, I watch *Jeopardy!*, *The Office*, *House M.D.*, and *MasterChef*. But generally, I enjoy whatever my little brother wants!

Stephen King's *The Dark Tower*, *House MD* the TV show

RuPaul's Drag Race shows the immense creativity of queer culture while simultaneously showing the vulnerability and the selective family aspect of queer men. For music, my favorite genre is pop punk; the fast guitars and drums and pop melodramatic melodies like The Front Bottoms is my go-to on Spotify.

My dad always played Lucky Dube's music in the house. I still remember dancing with him to " Ding Ding Licky Licky Licky Bong". Despite all the pain he caused, those carefree moments always come to mind when I think of him.

On my playlist, Dube is always on repeat.

The rustling of crusty leaves in the breeze; the sweet lullaby of finches and chickadees; the rhythmic crunch of loose gravel under my purple hiking boots—I love listening to the tranquil melody of the Colorado back—country, the song that never ceases to call to me.

Read: "Bury My Heart at Wounded Knee", "The Elements of Differential Geometry", "Life,

Death, and Neurosurgery", "Justice: What's The Right Thing to Do", "How Not To Die" (nutrition book)

Listen: EDM, This American Life, Planet Money, The Majority Report, Joe Rogan Podcast

Watch: Planet Earth, Mathologer, Rae's Medical School Vlogs

Read: *By the River Piedra I sat down and wept*, *The Book Thief*, Quora, *New York Times*, *Wired*

Watch: *Brooklyn Nine-nine*, *That 70s Show*, *How I Met Your Mother*, *Game of Thrones*, *Clueless*, Trevor Noah

Listen: J Cole, Kanye West, Frank Sinatra, Don Williams, Kenny Rogers, George Ezra, Janelle Monáe

Read: Any book by Murakami, any kind of comic, books with fairies and/or a sarcastic female lead

Listen: Christmas Music, because it's the closest I get to celebrating Christmas

Watch: *Elementary*, any house renovation show on the BBC network, *Brooklyn 99*, documentaries about north korea or sea creatures

Watch: International television shows and movies, because it's interesting to learn about different cultures (fun fact, some schools in China have hot water fountains rather than cold ones)

Listen: BTS, online sermons

Read: Funny Amazon reviews and classics like *Fahrenheit 451*, but I want to read more from Toni Morrison.

I watch *Doctor Who*. And read about it. And listen to the soundtracks. I also like to read about computers and space and psychology and political science and science fiction and murder mysteries and detective stories and lots and lots of fanfiction. But mostly *Doctor Who*.

When the choice is mine, I love watching Sunday football with my family. The smell of chili, the warmth of my lucky sweatshirt, the family cheers, and our dogs wearing orange Bronco jerseys are unforgettable experiences that I will miss when I start school at Stanford next Fall.

READ: *The Economist*, *The Girl Who Saved the King of Sweden*, *Outliers*, *Chronicle of a Death Foretold*, *Vorkosigan* Saga, *Art of Modern Calligraphy*

LISTEN: Radiolab podcasts, LAUV, HONNE, The Swan (Saint-Saens), Rhapsody in Blue (Gershwin), Beatles, ABBA, Hamilton soundtrack

WATCH: *Last Week Tonight*, *The Daily Show*, Comedians (Noah, Koy, Mulaney)

East of Eden—From the characters to Steinbeck's word choice, every detail contributes to this masterpiece

Anything by ABBA—Their tunes always put a smile on my face

Third Rock From The Sun—Every hilarious episode points out the "normal" antics that humans do on a daily basis

Slam poetry, Postmodern Jukebox Jazz, WIRED, TedED riddles, BYU Vocal point, 2Cellos, Vsauce, The Pianoguys, Jeopardy, SoulPancake, Solfa, The New Yorker, Kurt Hugo Schneider, Narcos, Anna Karenina by Tolstoy, The Republic by Plato, The Prince by Machiavelli, The Three Body Problem by Cixin Liu, Cinda Williams Chima, John Flanagan

When I have free time, which is quite rare, I love to sit down and read a good dystopian or romance novel. I also love listening to kpop; reading and connecting with the lyrics of artists halfway across the world has always amazed and excited me.

I'm a journalism junkie.

I both enter and exit sleep gripping my phone with CNN illuminating its screen.

The opening sequence to The Daily subconsciously stimulates my thoughts through Classical Conditioning.

I cannot help but to break out in dance to the NPR piano interludes.

The New York Times, The New Yorker, The Daily, Fresh Air, documentaries, Drake, Young Thug, Big Sean, Jase Harley, Jeopardy, classical music, non-fiction books on feminism or race, Vox, contemporary poetry, A Boogie Wit Da Hoodie, Picture Atlantic, The Beatles, Fader, Genius, Stanford Politics, The Mountain View High School Oracle

Read: *The Da Vinci Code*, *Frankenstein's Cat*, *Outliers*, *Tuesdays with Morrie*, John Grisham, *Mr. Monk* series, and subtitles on anything I watch

Listen: Maroon5, Vance Joy, EDM, Coldplay, Matt Maeson, The Score, Sugar Ray

Watch: *The Office*, *Blue Planet*, *American President*, *Good Will Hunting*, *Miss Congeniality*, PBS *NOVA*, *Breaking Bad*

Read: Refinery29, *Le Monde*, the *New York Times*, *The Sympathizer*, *The Family Fang*, *Midnight in the Garden of Good and Evil*, *Gone Girl*

Listen: French rap, Kendrick Lamar, the Mamma Mia soundtrack, Lorde, Alt-J, classic rock.

Watch: *Arrested Development*, the *West Wing*, John Mulaney, 90s thrillers, Wes Anderson movies

For emotionally complex melodies with a metanarrative: Mitski.

For the intersection of music, poetry, and truth: Noname.

For stream of consciousness jazz-hip hop: Sen Morimoto.

For when no one else is around: Disney Channel Original Movie soundtracks

"Quotes for Nasty Women" is my go to book for words of motivation and wisdom.

While driving, I listen to motivational TedTalks or various styles of Latino music like Mariachi, Huapango, or Corridos.

Documentaries to learn about new cultures and the conditions of oppressed populations.

Favorite journalism: *National Geographic, Time, NYT*. I absorb the blog *Wait But Why* & Quora. Creative muse: Pinterest. Binge-watched: Ted-Ed, *The Office*, *Orange is the New Black*. My nose is in these books:

Gang Leader For a Day, *Freakonomics*, and the hilarious *Hyperbole and a Half*. Archie comics are my childhood.

Being on a small island, attending Hawaii Symphony Orchestra's concerts is easily accessible and something I take advantage of regularly. When I listen, I hear no difference between them and the New York Philharmonic. To me their sound is equally beautiful, yet they are not on the same level of prestige.

Looking Forward To Stanford

Name one thing you are looking forward to experiencing at Stanford.

The What

In fifty words, tell Stanford *why* you want to attend Stanford. Is it to take classes from a particular professor? Or is it to join a club that focuses on sustainability?

The Why

Why would Stanford accept someone who isn't looking forward to attending? Admissions officers like to see students who know at least a little bit of research about the University before applying. You don't have to have visited the campus, but you should have a basic idea of what Stanford's about.

The Pitfalls

Sometimes applicants like to look up particular labs or research institutions at Stanford and write about them. Unless you're extremely familiar with the type of research that a particular organization does (and are genuinely fascinated by it), we don't recommend mentioning it. Admissions officers are not familiar with every research organization inside the University.

Additionally, try to stay away from cliché topics like the campus and activities like fountain hopping. It's easy to tell if an applicant actually know about the University, or if they just looked up sample responses on Google. Moreover, make sure you write about something unique to Stanford. (Frat parties are definitely not unique to Stanford.)

The How

Choose something unique. There's a place on campus for every activity imaginable. Ideally, you should write about something that you genuinely interested in. If you know of a smaller club or group that fits your interests exactly, write about it!

Sample I

Socially, I'm eagerly anticipating cornerstone campus traditions like the UC Berkeley-Stanford rivalry, getting trapped in the circle of death, and fountain hopping. Academically, I'm looking forward to engaging in high-level research with acclaimed professors and advancing my humanities education so I can develop an interdisciplinary view on the world's issues.

Sample II

The innovative spirit and the excitement that drips through every interaction at Stanford is something I look forward to experiencing. I want to connect with passionate people who do what they do because they like doing it, not because they're seeking a high salary.

Sample III

Working as a ticket sales associate for Stanford Athletics has allowed me to experience football games from the outside, but I want to know what it's like when Stanford is my school. I look forward to dancing to "All Right Now" alongside LSJUMB and celebrating the next Big Game win.

Sample IV

A hub for vibrant conversations, (generally) warm weather, and opportunities in fields I've never imagined existed. This represents such a stark contrast from where I live now, but it's a change I'm so looking forward to.

Sample V

The student-led "creative ecosystem" at Stanford's Institute for Diversity in the Arts doesn't exist at any other school. Both in and out of class, I'll be able to collaborate with other artists-scholars, study intersectionality, and cultivate an art practice that advocates for marginalized voices and fosters cultural change.

An Extra Hour

Imagine you had an extra hour in the day—how would you spend that time?

The What

In fifty words, tell Stanford *why* you want to attend Stanford. Is it to take classes from a particular professor? Or is it to join a club that focuses on sustainability?

The Why

Why would Stanford accept someone who isn't looking forward to attending? Admissions officers like to see students who know at least a little bit of research about the University before applying. You don't have to have visited the campus, but you should have a basic idea of what Stanford's about.

The Pitfalls

Sometimes applicants like to look up particular labs or research institutions at Stanford and write about them. Unless you're extremely familiar with the type of research that a particular organization does (and are genuinely fascinated by it), we don't recommend mentioning it. Admissions officers are not familiar with every research organization inside the University.

Additionally, try to stay away from cliché topics like the campus and activities like fountain hopping. It's easy to tell if an applicant actually know about the University, or if they just looked up sample responses on Google. Moreover, make sure you write about something unique to Stanford. (Frat parties are definitely not unique to Stanford.)

The How

Choose something unique. There's a place on campus for every activity imaginable. Ideally, you should write about something that you genuinely interested in. If you know of a smaller club or group that fits your interests exactly, write about it!

Sample I

Every breathing cell in me wants to answer more sleep! But after we've all adjusted clocks, those extra 2.5 minutes-per-hour slowly fade into routine life. Realistically, an hour isn't enough to make world peace, but I could use those minutes to drink my water and properly hydrate.

Sample II

"Everyone has 24 hours in a day, even Bill Gates." – Mom. Frankly, it'd be wasteful to keep an extra hour of traveling, creating, and learning to myself. After discovering my advantage over Bill Gates, I'd use it to figure out how I can help others also get an extra hour.

Sample III

What are the restrictions? Does everyone get an hour or just me? Is it a solid hour or can I break it up? Can I stop time? Are there consequences? What about gravity and other laws of nature—still working? This question has far too many possibilities.

More realistically: sleep.

Sample IV

25 hours per day? If there really was an extra hour, the world would be chaos. With the ecosystem turning upside down and Earth practically engulfed in flames, I would spend that 25th-hour building a rocket ship so I could move to Mars and get away from this mayhem.

Sample V

The student-led "creative ecosystem" at Stanford's Institute for Diversity in the Arts doesn't exist at any other school. Both in and out of class, I'll be able to collaborate with other artists-scholars, study intersectionality, and cultivate an art practice that advocates for marginalized voices and fosters cultural change.

Elaborate on an Extracurricular

Please briefly elaborate on one of your extracurricular activities or work experiences.

The fact that this essay exists is great—it frees up real estate in other essays, and gives you an explicit place to expound on what you've been involved in. Pick one activity, and talk about not just what you've achieved, but what you've learned, and how you've grown.

Here are how some of our applicants have done it:

Sample I

As part of Hispanic Society, I feel proud of the culture that I know. Hispanic Society is an inclusive, service-based club and we do everything like river cleanups, natural disaster relief drives, food drives, and even volunteer as monsters in haunted houses. We spend Saturday mornings handing out food at a community pantry or staffing a city run or manning a booth at a festival, or we spend Thursdays after school serving meals in a homeless shelter. I won't try to convince you I am selfless and altruistic or anything we all want to write in our college apps. But I will say that through this club I proudly serve my community with my friends as we prove to our city and to ourselves that being Hispanic can mean something positive. This club has helped me solidify my identity as a proud Latino student for change.

Sample II

I have come to more deeply understand the truism "You don't truly understand something until you have to explain it to someone else." As I was completing the AP Physics curriculum through my self-study of the topic as a ninth grader, I read many books and guides. I became increasingly dissatisfied with the rote nature of presentation in many of these resources. The problems in these books simply required plugging in numbers and memorizing formulas. So, I began collecting examples. With the power of TeX, I compiled them into a book, which is now published ([NAME'S] Guide to AP Physics C: Mechanics). Writing can be solitary and difficult. It required persistence, with six months of daily work, and iterative effort to key in on what I really wanted to say. I found it extremely rewarding and plan to continue writing as a way to understand and communicate complex ideas effectively.

Sample III

Glossophobia is the term for a "fear of public speaking". Though 200 million people suffer from it … I most certainly DON'T. On the contrary, I adore public speaking. I discovered Speech and Debate during my Freshman year and I have been on the team since. Undoubtedly, it is my favorite extracurricular activity in high school. I held an officer position during all four years on the team. For the first three years, I was the Historian. My duties included marketing activities such as creating fundraiser ads, completely redesigning our website, and archiving the team's awards after each tournament. I've been the Interpretation Lead for the last three years. In this role, I am a coach, mentor, and manager to my fellow teammates who also compete in

Interpretation Events. I aspire to be an active member of the Stanford Debate team and to continue competing in college.

Sample IV

No matter how hard I train, I will never win my 200-meter race. But as competitive as I am in the rest of my life, this surprisingly doesn't bother me.

At track meets, I fly as my spikes dig into the soft rubber, propelling me forward. Everything melts away—there are no thoughts, no sounds. Left, right, I sprint down the straightaway. My lungs begin to burn. I press on, pushing myself to the limit. The finish line approaches and I lunge across. Reality rushes back, but the exhilaration remains.

According to Ricky Bobby, "If you ain't first, you're last!" But I guess Ricky Bobby never ran track.

After all, if I followed his logic, I'd be "last" every time I ran. But for me, track is about the thrill of the race, knowing that as long as I give it my all, I can never truly lose.

Profiles

Below, we've included profiles from five current Stanford undergrads, complete with activity lists, comments, numerical scores, and our own analysis.

Profile I

Colorado

Personal Essay

My eyes lock with those of Maestro Kenney as his baton plunges, signaling the downbeat and what should be the euphonious emergence of my trumpet's song. In my head, I can hear Maestro's deep, cavernous voice: "Play with swagger!" As a composed orchestral trumpet player, I would never use the word 'swagger' to describe myself, nor expect my professional Maestro to demand it from me. But I have to trust him to successfully portray the pompous Toreador and flirtatious Carmen from Bizet's opera at the upcoming concert. I take a sip of water and then raise my trumpet, trying to embody exactly what my white-haired Maestro envisions.

After dress rehearsal, I watch as each orchestral player floods backstage, bustling around like a hive of worker bees. Within this chaos, my eyes linger over to a cellist as she struggles to simultaneously grasp her instrument and other possessions. I can see the inevitable—that her precarious balance will collapse. We had never talked before, but her relatable predicament invites my empathy. So, without pausing, I set down my water bottle to lend her a hand. She quickly thanks me, and we are both buzzing out of our backstage chambers with the crowd.

Halfway home from the hall, with the warmth of the music still beating through my veins, I realize that the unthinkable has happened: I have lost my water bottle. With the cellist's sudden need for help and Maestro's perplexing demand consuming my thoughts, I forgot to grab my bottle before rushing out from backstage.

Even though it is merely a scratched, plastic bottle, I feel genuinely upset losing it. That bottle had sustained me through years of 100 degree F soccer games; it quenched me and my bamboo plant during the 10-hour-long days of my atmospheric science internship; and it propelled me on my 14,000 foot ascent up Grays and Torreys Peaks. On the surface, this water bottle might merely be cheap plastic, yet it shared my life's happiest memories and accompanied me on my difficult journeys. I feel like I lost a part of my identity along with that bottle.

But the show must go on. A week later at the final performance, as I am submerged under the blinding stage lights, Maestro Kenney's voice echoes through my mind once more, supplanting any lingering thoughts over my lost bottle. I need to embrace Carmen's 'swagger' through my trumpet—I need to make my Maestro, and myself, proud.

With passionate determination, I raise my trumpet and lock into the continuous march of Maestro's baton. My dynamic trumpet solo reso-nates throughout the hall, finally unveiling Carmen's 'swagger' as she and the Toreador swirl around me. Her red, gitana dress mirrors my crescendos while she dances flirtatiously to my intricate rhythms. Our outpouring of passion continues to escalate until, at long last, "To-reador, L'amour t'attend—love awaits you!" As our last chord echoes throughout the auditorium, I look over to Maestro Kenney once more, to his proud smile and tear-filled eyes, and know that I successfully animated the vivacious Carmen through a few feet of metal tubing.

As applause floods the hall, strangely enough, my mind returns to my water bottle. I realize my water bottle never defined my identity—I merely lost a replaceable piece of blue plastic. Instead, I can see that music's unwavering beat drives my heart as I pursue each of my passions. A Tchaikovsky symphony runs through my head as I chase the soccer ball. Latin sambas traverse my office as I investigate the uncharted Antarctic climate. Nature's tranquil song accompanies me to the Rocky Mountain summits. And when I take the stage, with musical passion surrounding me, I feel most alive. I become my authentic self.

Through music, I unleash my intrinsic 'swagger.'

Intellectual Vitality

"Y nadie mas que yo determinara mi futuro," Lydia dramatically declared as the oh-so-familiar "jugar el siguiente episodio" (play next episode) box appeared on the bottom of the screen. Instinctively, I clicked on Netflix's infamous button, and proceeded to watch the next episode of my favorite telenovela, *Las Chicas del Cable* (Cable Girls). Was I binge-watching an addictive telenovela? Sure. But was I also improving my Spanish speaking and comprehension, and preparing for the upcoming AP Spanish exam? Definitely.

After watching the episodios pilotos (pilot episodes) for each telenovela type in class, I became immediately intrigued by the historicas (historical telenovelas). Even though I had plenty of other assignments to do, I rationalized my desire to watch the next episode: Spanish culture and history fascinated me, and I knew that any exposure to the Spanish language outside of the classroom would quickly improve my own Spanish abilities. Before I knew it, I had finished both seasons of *Las Chicas del Cable*, and had already become engrossed in *El Tiempo Entre Costuras* (The Time in Between), another telenovela histórica centered on fierce Spanish women in the 19205. While this might not have been the wisest or most conventional study method for the AP exam, in retrospect, it was perfectly ideal as I got a 5 and developed a passion for Spanish history and language outside of the classroom. And ¡Dios Mio! I just discovered a new season of *Las Chicas del Cable*!

Roommate Essay

I have a confession to make: I hate chocolate. It is perfectly under-standable if you judge me as an oddity (as my own grandparents even do), but I can't think of a better way for you to get to know me than through my most controversial, non-political opinions. In all of the clubs and activities in which I hold a leadership position, I al-ways pose the ice-breaker question: what is your most controversial, non-political opinion? I relish seeing my peers' faces when I tell them that even though I enjoy baking addictive brownies, decadent choc-olate eclairs, and perfectly-chewy chocolate-chip cookies, the 'sweet aroma' of chocolate disgusts me. Or that I also love waking up early— to me, there is no better time of the day than 4 am, when a silent tran-quility rests in the air as the world remains in slumber. Or that I don't mind spiders, and even try to rescue them from the fatal, stomping boots of others. In fact, I would be happy to protect you from every menacing, eight-eyed, eight-legged arachnid by being the designat-ed spider-taker-outer for our dorm (you're welcome in advance). So, what is your most controversial, non-political opinion?

What is Meaningful to You?

As I walk through the school hallways, everyone turns and smiles longingly at me. They must smell the sweet aroma of the tin-foil-wrapped treats resting in my hands. After three years of baking for friends, clubs, and teachers, I have developed a distinct reputation—specifically for my macarons, eclairs, decorated shortbread, and mini-muffins. I love the creative opportunities I discover as I plug in my electric mixer, resulting in Hello-Kitty-decorated macarons for my Hello-Kitty-obsessed Spanish teacher and a realistic geode cake for my Link freshmen. I embrace the technical complexities of complicated recipes and the artistic freedom of edible masterpieces.

Even though many people stress over beeping timers, footless or cracked macarons, and the daunting task of cleaning up, I have always found baking to be quite relaxing.

What is the most significant challenge that society faces today?

Watching helplessly as ping-pong-ball-sized hail decimated our garden, record-breaking hurricanes devastated the Southeast, and wildfires fueled by unusually-severe drought and Santa Ana Winds ravaged California, I'm constantly reminded of the escalating threat of global climate change and worse, denial of it. Averting further climate change is society's most critical challenge.

How did you spend your last two summers?

From wandering on accidental 9-mile hikes, to trying veganism (and sticking with it); from persevering through online swimming (I'm a human anchor), to exploring Antarctic snow accumulation and sublimation via my internship, my last two summers have consisted of nonstop, frequently-unexpected adventures (plus countless hours of trumpet practice).

What historical moment or event do you wish you could have witnessed?

November 20,1982. Stanford's win against Cal seems imminent, so trumpet in hand, I rush onto the field with the band. Suddenly, the Cal player carrying the football sprints towards me. Thanks to my years of soccer training, I slide-tackle him, preventing that infamous touchdown—"it's all right now, baby."

What five words best describe you?

Renaissance (wo)man, proactive, empathetic, determined, human GPS

When the choice is yours, what do you read, listen to, or watch?

The rustling of crusty leaves in the breeze; the sweet lullaby of finches and chickadees; the rhythmic crunch of loose gravel under my purple hiking boots—I love listening to the tranquil melody of the Colorado back-country, the song that never ceases to call to me.

Name one thing you are looking forward to experiencing at Stanford.

The spotlight illuminates me standing proudly in center stage as my trumpet's sound begins to resonate throughout the hall. The orchestra enters behind me, supporting my melody and fully animating the silent space. I cannot wait to perform at Bing Concert Hall, harmonizing with academically brilliant student-musicians.

Imagine you had an extra hour in the day—how would you spend that time?

I would add an hour between 4 and 5 am, while everything is silent. Whether spent running on the elliptical as I watch Crash Course Biology videos, or playing Charlier Etudes on my trumpet, every minute of my early-morning prime-time would be used for personal growth and rejuvenation.

Elaborate on EC/Work experience

Last summer, I collaborated with scientists at the National Center for Atmospheric Research (NCAR) as a paid Pre-Collegiate Intern. As part of NCAR's large-scale project studying Antarctic snow accumulation, I analyzed snowfall data and weather patterns from Alexander Tall Tower on the Ross Ice Shelf. Specifically, I identified trends in snow accumulation by classifying snowfall events as falling snow, blowing snow, or both. I also explored beyond the original research plan by identifying and analyzing snow sublimation. While scientists have accurately estimated Antarctic deglaciation rates, little is known about the mechanisms of snow accumulation and its impacts on this deglaciation. My work will help refine methods to measure snow accumulation in the future, and will enable scientists to include more precise accumulation measurements in climate models, improving their ability to predict rising sea levels. I was invited to present this work at the American Meteorological Society's National Conference in Arizona.

Activities

1. Research	National Center for Atmospheric Research Intern
12 Break 20 hr/wk, 6 wk/yr Continue	Selected from >40 applicants; research & analyze data on Antarctic Sublimation & Snow Accumulation; invited to present poster at AMS Nat'l Conference
2. Music: Instrumental	Orchestra, Trumpet Soloist
9, 10, 11, 12 Year 15 hr/wk, 45 wk/yr Continue	1st Chair All-State(2x); Nationally-acclaimed Young Artists Orchestra: performed solos in Mahler 5, Tchaikovsky 5, Bizet's Carmen, & Handel's Messiah
3. Music: Instrumental	Band, Trumpet 1st Chair and by Audition
9, 10, 11, 12 Year 10 hr/wk, 52 wk/yr Continue	All-State Band; CU & CSU Honor Bands; Colorado Honor Band: Section Leader, 1st chair in Symphony Winds, Student Board Member:plan fundraising & events
4. Athletics: JV/Varsity	Soccer, Varsity and Competitive Club
9, 10, 11, 12 Year 8 hr/wk, 40 wk/yr Continue	4 years HS Varsity, senior captain, top 16 HS team in CO; Rush Club team, played for 13 years, top 10-15 team in CO, Presidents Cup State Finalist 2x
5. Academic	National Honor Society Treasurer

11, 12 School 2 hr/wk, 35 wk/yr Continue	Lead tutor training; plan events & induction; improve Academic Workshop tutoring: help struggling students, relationship-building focus; bake treats
6. Community Service (Volunteer)	Link Commissioner and Link Leader
11, 12 School, Break 2 hr/wk, 40 wk/yr Continue	Run leadership training for 60 Link Leaders; plan Freshmen Orientation; year-long freshmen support; award student of the month; bake macarons & more
7. Science/Math	Math League Co-founder & Co-president
11, 12 School 2 hr/wk, 35 wk/yr Continue	Lead team of 15 in competitions and projects, such as designing math-themed Escape Room, which won 1st at CSU Math Day Comp; tutor all levels of math
8. Community Service (Volunteer)	Accountability Committees for District and School
10, 11, 12 School 2 hr/wk, 15 wk/yr Continue	1 of 5 students for District: provide key insights for policies, mental health support, post-grad pathways; Heritage HS: advise and support Principal
9. Community Service (Volunteer)	Community Relations, Fundraising Activity Chair

9, 10, 11, 12	Plan MAD Week fundraiser; I facilitated Solar Lamp donations to sister school in Sierra Leone (300 lamps) & Teacher-in-a-box (raised $800 in 3 hours)
School	
2 hr/wk, 14 wk/yr	
Continue	
10. Work (Paid)	Trumpet Instructor, Paid and Volunteer
9, 10, 11, 12	Teach private trumpet lessons for pay; student teacher for Colorado Honor Band; work individually teaching younger HS students theory, jazz, technique
Year	
3 hr/wk, 38 wk/yr	
Continue	

Reader 1

PE: fretting over lost water bottle — companion at soccer, internships, hikes — realizes after performance that music is what defines true self

IV: binging telenovelas on Netflix, improving Spanish and knowledge of culture/history

WM: baking and sharing the joyous results with others

EC: top tier due to FARF 1 for trumpet with nice comments. Lots of depth and leadership in band, soccer, and orchestra

PRIV: solid with PE about music defining authentic self and unique IV essay turning binging Netflix telenovelas into a positive.

Reader 2

Agree with R1 that [NAME] has a strong app

Strength at testing, academic performance, music

IV: no regards to chemistry... confusing... unsure what she wants to do

POE is definitely FARF at the moment

Tags

FARF

Reader 1 Scores	
Metric	**Score**
Test Rtg	1
HSR	2
Support	2
EC	1+
SP-IV	3
Eval	2+

Reader 2 Scores	
Metric	**Score**
Test Rtg	1
HSR	3
Support	3
EC	1
SP-IV	3
Eval	2-

The Story

A trumpet prodigy and a soccer star who's passionate about long-term environmental change.

The Evidence

It's clear that this applicant has exceptional talent with the trumpet—not only do they have three activities related to the trumpet, but they dedicated their personal essay to music, and mentioned the trumpet in multiple short essays. They submitted a musical supplement, and got a FARF 1 tag. Clearly, the dedication showed through, with the applicant receiving a rare 1+ for EC, with the first reader commenting, "EC: top tier due to FARF 1 for trumpet with nice comments. Lots of depth and leadership in band, soccer, and orchestra" and the second reader writing, "POE is definitely FARF at the moment." Soccer, and the applicant's other pursuits, received less attention—both in the application, and from the readers.

The Technique

This application is set up with a clear spike, music, but strong auxiliary pursuits; soccer and environmental research. However, the application also mentions several other pursuits that distract from the main message. There are no essays about leadership or community change, so the NHS, Link, and volunteering activities fall flat. The demonstration of an interest in environmental sustainability (through the research activity, which the applicant chose to elaborate on, as well as short essays on the Colorado backcountry and their last two summers) lines up well, but clashes with her intended major in Chemistry. All in all, an applicant with a strong spike, but an application which could be more cohesive.

Takeaways

If you're musically talented, showcase it; through essays, activities, and a supplement.

Match your application with your major (don't give your readers that "Why chemistry?" moment!)

The readers don't really care about your "minor" involvements (NHS, Math League).

Profile II

Philippines

Personal Essay

I tried to hold them back, but they escaped – tiny, iridescent pearls streaming towards the surface, shimmering with the rainbow prism of childish imagination. Irrepressible, they rushed in frenzied torrent upwards to the gleaming ceiling.

Amazingly, I reached the surface solid and whole, nothing missing except words snatched from my mouth by air currents. The only sounds ringing across the water were the bellows of my swimming coach and the splash-splash of other swimmers who failed to hold their breath in the water.

"Did you see?" My mind brimmed with details. "I built an underwater spa in my blub blub… were tea cakes and flowers and … blub blub blub… should have been there! It was blub … blub!"

"Stop talking and keep paddling!" Coach Hazel shouted, "you're going to drown!"

The youngest of five children, I always had to speak over the combined chatter of four older siblings. There was never enough time to express the ideas converging in my head; if I didn't tell them all now, I-would-never-be-able-to. I rush words. Consequently, our nightly jousts expanded my lung capacity, contributing to my reputation as the too-talkative member of the family.

It's no wonder that in high school, I threw myself into debate and theatre. Never lacking words, I defended opinions far-removed from my own, such as arguing for the use of police body cameras and protesting against the use of euthanasia. In theatre, I improvised my way through fantastical scenes, switching roles from Assistant Dale buying groceries, to Delilah a transgender ex-wife. I sharpened my hatchet of childhood bickering into a fine scalpel, expertly dissecting and contesting arguments, while fine-tuning my squeaky soprano to a modulated contralto. I used my voice.

When the great Theatre production began, I thought "Finally!" I will be heard as Beneatha Younger in A Raisin in the Sun: African American, highly ambitious, opinionated daughter – like me – who sought to speak her mind. Beneatha unleashed facets of my own persona. By lending my voice to another, my "relentless chatterbox" flaw emerged as a weapon for others.

As executive director of a musical charity event, I grew comfortable on a different type of stage, not as a performer but as a campaigner.

"25 raffle ticket packages will fund one boat!" I called out for fishermen in Iloilo who lost their livelihood to Typhoon Haiyan, raising enough money to build four boats through the NVC Peter Project. I spent my breaks asking people to trade their lunch money for tickets and calling companies to petition for sponsorships. Behind the scenes, I witnessed transformations that few else would see, every scrap of ticket sold multiplying as pages of books, slowly filling up the new library at Buting Elementary School.

Involvement provided me an understanding of others' silent stories and made me realize that my voice can be used for those who have no voice in society. In every community I encounter, from the packed elementary classrooms in Tagaytay to the streets of Manila, I listen for the intersection of voices, allowing my voice to intermingle with the shrieks of "takbo!" and "pahingi po".

I no longer struggle to out-do anyone in speaking; instead I create ripples in my school, my society and its many communities by reaching out and connecting to those around me. I serve as a megaphone, amplifying others' voices when they are drowned out by cute animal videos, clickbait articles, and your cousin's fiance's latest beach photos.

I came to understand that being listened to is not about raising your voice and elevating your own perspective, but giving light to the lives of others whose stories are hidden. I hear other people's narratives and act on their behalf. If I engulf myself in a sea of stories, a diverse community will be nourished within and grow around me to create better lives – voices louder together.

Intellectual Vitality

Stuart joined me in a *butiki*-hunting (Asian gecko) expedition. On that fateful night when I caught one in my toothbrush holder, I watched as he deliberately cut the tiny gecko's tail in the name of science. "It'll grow back," he reassured me, "watch how the tail still wiggles. It has a life of its own."

With this same morbid fascination, I viewed the dissection of a cow's eye in Biology class, ten years later, mesmerized by dismantling and reorganizing living organisms into components, then coalescing them into new configurations and creations.

I learned to break down mathematical equations into complex derivatives, integrating them to new hierarchies of existence. Numbers propagate in my head, compelling me to dismantle and marry 20 to

70 and 3 to 7, before putting them together as the perfect square of 100. I thrill at tackling the big and complex, tabulating them into neat compartments of knowledge and application, arriving at a synergistic whole.

I organize groups of people based on characteristics to form the optimum attack squads. From teaching teams in PREP to councils within BOB, I can recognize people's strengths and qualities to recast them to my version of the Golden Ratio: where the proportion of scientists to creatives in a group mirrors the fraction of a student's attention span in a class period.

I seek to discover and reformulate Golden Ratios in the slivers of the world around me. Every component can take a life of its own, just like the butiki's tail.

Roommate Essay

Kamusta ka!

What languages do you speak? I know English, Mandarin, Tagalog, and a dash from every country I've visited.

Hungry? "*Gutom ako*": it's how I define myself – a voracious consumer of food and ideas—which I down indiscriminately—hankering for beef tapa with garlic rice and chasing down information about Romanov tsars on Wikipedia. I'm curious to know your predilections and the words you communicate them by.

Growing up, I decoded my siblings' dialects (from caffeine-deprived grumbles to whale noises); knowing the difference between tired, hungry, and "hangry" spelled the difference between strategic retreat and offerings of food. I hope to learn the language of our friendship:

from your early morning just-woke-up sounds, to the pitch of your favorite 80's song! The language of Stanford awaits us in the stories of our peers.

I explore worlds and experiences. When my family traveled to Hong Kong, I waved goodbye to a Turkish gentleman in the elevator with "Allahaısmarladık!", and the door closed on his baffled and bemused expression. Shall we be Armstrong and Aldrin together, taking confident strides into alien worlds? Let's step into White Plaza and find co-conspirators at the activities fair, venture into ENGR 40M and build a lightbox, learn how to transform our foxtrot into a waltz in Roble Gym.

To everyone we meet along the way, let's say "hello" in your language and mine! We can chisel away at the unfamiliarity of a new home with the shared speech of food, love, and laughter.

[NAME]

What is Meaningful to You?

"Anak, gising na. Kailangan mong uminom ng gamot." (Wake up, my child. You need to drink your medicine.)

With absolute trust I followed Ate Merly as she ministered a cool cloth to cut through my feverish haze. In that moment, I noted red veins in her eyes and dark shadows beneath. 3 am: she had been up 36 hours caring for me.

Six years later, Ate Merly – surrogate mother, friend, protector – was diagnosed with cancer. When I recall her life, I read through chapters of love and sacrifice. Ate Merly's sacrifice stems from her heart, a life fully dedicated to caring.

I appreciate unconditional sacrifice: my mom juggling work and a household of five children, my sister patiently teaching me how to bump a volleyball, teachers staying late after class to explain challenging concepts. All performed with no expectation of return.

When viewed against all that, it's easy to give up my long weekends to teach fifth and sixth grade classes in rural Tagaytay. I no longer sigh when my mom asks me to accompany her to weekly mass; no more complaints when I have to wait an extra hour for my sister after work.

For Ate Merly, and for everyone who doesn't have an Ate Merly, I take action and make my own little offerings, inserting pages of love and care in other people's narratives.

Sacrifice is a meaningful expression of love.

What is the most significant challenge that society faces today?

Education for empowerment and freedom:

The nature of education has changed from being knowledge-driven to serving socio-political needs, ie. colonization, industrialization, technology.

The challenge is democratizing education and removing barriers to access, allowing choices that truly empower the individual, regardless of social perceptions and affiliations.

How did you spend your last two summers?

2018:

Teach for Philippines, Data Impact and Assessment Intern; Stanford, brother's graduation; Saint Petersburg, historical immersion in dazzling Romanov structures "built on spilled blood"; Organized service trip to rural Tagaytay: taught at 5 elementary schools

2017:

Focus Global Inc, Marketing Intern; Organized volleyball camp for students from 6 different schools

What historical moment or event do you wish you could have witnessed?

1842: Ada Lovelace's process of writing the first computer programming algorithm.

I want to ask her how she envisioned people and society collaborating with technology as a tool, and understand how she was able to imagine beyond the bounds of her own reality.

What five words best describe you?

Forward-looking, hustle-and-heart, link, sparkplug, loudspeaker

When the choice is yours, what do you read, listen to, or watch?

READ: The Economist, The Girl Who Saved the King of Sweden, Outliers, Chronicle of a Death Foretold, Vorkosigan Saga, Art of Modern Calligraphy

LISTEN: Radiolab podcasts, LAUV, HONNE, The Swan (Saint-Saens), Rhapsody in Blue (Gershwin), Beatles, ABBA, Hamilton soundtrack

WATCH: Last Week Tonight, The Daily Show, Comedians (Noah, Koy, Mulaney)

Name one thing you are looking forward to experiencing at Stanford.

Birthing and launching ideas to reality.

From ideation: exploring the d.school to learn different ways of approaching problems.

To gestation: tinkering in room 64 and the PRL to prototype my plans.

To conception: where I inevitably meet failure! Re-think my plans, disassemble my thoughts, and recreate my brainchild. Iterate.

Imagine you had an extra hour in the day—how would you spend that time?

Indulge in the beautiful mess of creative expression: trade in my rulers and TI-84 for a brush pen and colorful inks to perfect the art of calligraphy, tracing thin upward strokes to satiate an artistic itch, boldly sweeping thick downward strokes that capture elegance in a written word.

Elaborate on EC/Work experience

"Ooh"s and "ahh"s filled the room; I had created a source of wonder. It was my first PREP trip to Bulalo Elementary School, and children marveled at the kaleidoscope of colors spread on their classroom floor. I too was captivated. Not by the color-changing red cabbage pH indicator in plastic cups around the room, but by the students' utter fascination. A craving for the spectacular was born in me.

Following that trip, I spent every week before PREP trips turning my kitchen into an amateur chemistry lab, attempting to concoct new potions to make my students fall in love with learning. I was a wizard brewing baking soda and vinegar, painting the electromagnetic spectrum of the rainbow with scientific witchcraft.

The genuine enthusiasm of my students at Bulalo fired my own curiosity and fueled intrepid innovations, showing me just how magical learning is when shared with others.

Activities

1. Community Service (Volunteer)	Promoting Rural Education in the PH, President
10, 11, 12 Year 48 hr/wk, 5 wk/yr Continue	Organize 5 yearly trips to schools in rural Philippines; lead student teams to independently create interactive lesson plans for elementary students.
2. Community Service (Volunteer)	ISM Battle of the Bands, Executive Director
10, 11, 12 Year, Break 2 hr/wk, 32 wk/yr Continue	Manage 2 annual service-musical events with over 800 attendees; raised ₱1.6M ($30k USD) and ₱1.3M ($24k USD) in 2017 and 2018 to donate to charities.
3. Athletics: JV/Varsity	ISM Varsity Badminton, Co-Captain

9, 10, 11, 12 Year 12 hr/wk, 12 wk/yr Continue	Received the MVP award and led the team as co-captain in 2018; participated in an Interscholastic Association of Southeast Asian Schools competition.
4. Athletics: JV/Varsity	ISM Varsity Volleyball
9, 10, 11, 12 Year 12 hr/wk, 12 wk/yr Continue	Participated in two Interscholastic Association of Southeast Asian Schools competition; won the silver medal in 2017.
5. Internship	Teach for the Philippines, Data Analysis Intern
11 Break 20 hr/wk, 4 wk/yr	Data Impact and Assessment: scraped and digitized student information from Philippine public school records to implement a standardized database.
6. Community Service (Volunteer)	Estancia Elementary School: Fundraising Project
12 Year 1 hr/wk, 12 wk/yr	Organized traditional Filipino "boodle fight" to fundraise and collect donations for new sports equipment and funding for elementary school programs.
7. Community Service (Volunteer)	ICARE Outreach Program
9, 10, 11, 12 Year 60 hr/wk, 1 wk/yr Continue	Participate in annual International Community Actively Responding to the Environment program with rural communities in Botolan, Antipolo, Estancia.

8. Academic	National Honor Society
10, 11, 12 Year 2 hr/wk, 4 wk/yr Continue	Promotes scholarship and leadership throughout ISM; assisting in annual events such as Teacher Appreciation Day and fundraising for Operation Smile.
9. Academic	National Chinese Honor Society
11, 12 Year 2 hr/wk, 4 wk/yr	Founding member of the inaugural chapter in ISM. Encourages members' lifelong learning to gain a better understanding of Chinese language and culture.

Reader 1

Very competitive high school load, taking 4 Higher Level classes

Had a few missed opportunities in her writing

Standard depth writing, left me wanting more

PE & IVE were a little choppy and hard to connect, but the PE was more solid—didn't get a good sense of IV

Lots of notable comserv initiatives but still EC 3

Context is key here and will play a part

Reader 2

PE is solid, IVE is more scattered

IV is standard, present in PE & R1 highlights

She can do the work and is driven

ECs more standard, impact can be seen within campus community

Not seeing clear POE

Recommendation: leaning in

Not sure enough is here but leaning in slightly for context; can see a case but not sure if it's enough for her to emerge

Reader 3

Dean Read

Tags

L, OD, SIBL

Reader 1 Scores	
Metric	**Score**
Test Rtg	1
HSR	3
Support	3
EC	3
SP-IV	3
Eval	3+

Reader 2 Scores	
Metric	**Score**
Test Rtg	1
HSR	3
Support	2
EC	3
SP-IV	3
Eval	2-

The Story

A thoughtful, community-minded student with polished essays and lots of volunteer work.

The Evidence

This applicant centered her application around community work and structured her extracurricular activities around that focus. Although her extracurricular activities don't particularly stand out, she made sure to list activities that pair well with her essays, such as organizing multiple educational trips to rural Philippines. This student's admissions tags show that she is also a Legacy and Sibling Legacy admit—both Readers 1 and 2 make a note of that fact, saying that her "context" will play a role in the final decision.

The Technique

The application is very coherent, painting a picture of the student as introspective, caring, and engaged. Although her application was boosted by her special status as a Legacy applicant, there is no doubt that the quality of several of her essays helped push her over the edge and get accepted. As noted by the readers, there were several areas on her applications that appeared to be lacking, but the overall cohesiveness of her essays and activities successfully portray her as a strong candidate with a strong commitment to helping her community. Though she listed athletic activities for both her second and third activities, she didn't expand on them in her essays. Had she highlighted those athletic commitments in conjunction with her community work, her application would have been stronger as a whole.

Takeaways

Make sure every piece of your application sticks together.

Profile III

California

Personal Essay

My earliest childhood memories are of witnessing the abuse that occurred at home. My memories of my father split into two different personalities. One side was the loving parent who loved me like daddy's little girl, and the other side couldn't control his anger so he took it out on his wife and child. As I grew older the abuse became life threatening. I feared for my Mom's life and longed for the loving father I remembered. When I was 13 years old my father threatened to assault my mother with a knife in his hand. After this encounter I had to do what was best for my Mom and me even if it meant breaking up our family. After school I encouraged my Mom to tell our family friends what was happening, and we never came back home to my father. A month later I saw him again when he tried to convince me to make us stay, "If mama leaves me, you'll never have enough money to make it to college." I wasn't phased. I knew it simply wasn't true. I have kept this thought with me to prove him wrong because I know I'm capable of succeeding.

When my mother and I lived alone, we became a team. Due to her language barrier I had to grow up quickly to help understand the bills and translate for her during her conversations with bosses or the landlord. Without my father's income my mother had to find more work. My mother has worked as a housekeeper all my life, but now that I am older her struggles resonated with me more. She was only educated up to the 3rd grade in Guatemala, and here I am with the opportunity of a free K-12 education and a future college education, if I apply myself. This realization gave me a new found motivation in school to take advantage of the opportunity I have to educate myself.

I began to see my education as a source of power. Education became my resistance against the odds. My motivation to succeed was inspired by wanting to honor my mother's sacrifices but also within myself. I want to challenge myself and give back to the world.

For two years my father and I worked to rebuild our relationship. Although we still had a lot to work on I felt like his little girl again. I had my loving father back.

During Thanksgiving break 2016, doctors diagnosed my father with Stage 4 liver cancer. I tried my best to take advantage of my time left with him and used my academics as a coping mechanism to honor him. We celebrated his final birthday at 75 years young, my final birthday with him at 16 years old, and our last Christmas together. I saw my father pass away in the hospital on December 28, 2016.

His death gave me gratitude for my life and opportunities. After his death I pushed myself even harder in academics and extracurriculars. I found a new drive that has changed who I am and what I aspire to be.

Almost two years later, in the summer of 2018, I received a scholarship to go to CCL's International conference in Washington, D.C. and lobby on Capitol Hill. I came back home with the secret dream of wanting to become a congress member or senator. I quickly dismissed it because I doubted myself.

For the next few weeks I thought about how my father's death impacted me. I realized I had no reason to silence my own dreams. My father reminds me how precious life is and to keep in mind that I have the opportunity to leave this world a little bit better than when I found it.

That is what gives me the confidence to proudly state my once silent dream of one day becoming a congress member or senator.

Intellectual Vitality

My greatest curiosity started with a misconception. I believed that signing was a universal language. All of my life my parents have been hard of hearing, but neither had the chance to learn a signed language.

In the summer of 2015 our family friend, Elaine Colett, found a program at my community college offering courses to high school juniors and seniors. I was a rising freshman, so when we asked if I could apply, nine people told us no. However, the 10th person said maybe, and we took that maybe with us. I was allowed to take two courses that summer.

This was the perfect opportunity to explore my new found curiosity in American Sign Language (ASL).

I was originally drawn to the Deaf community because I was in awe and curious of the language. These past four years of study have taught me the depth of visual languages and Deaf culture.

Seeing my Deaf peers and professors being constantly denied their basic human right to communication drives me to be a continuous advocate and an ally for the Deaf community.

I've put this knowledge to use and formed the ASL Club at my community college. I am starting to get involved with some of the intersectionality in the Deaf community starting with the DeafBlind community.

I continue to learn because when a community teaches me I can thank them by giving back. Making me feel like I have contributed something positive with my new knowledge.

Roommate Essay

Dear future friend,

Feel free to walk on my side of the room. Communication and respect are something I value dearly. I enjoy learning about other people's perspectives and viewpoints especially when it comes to culture or politics. But respect will always be maintained, as my Mom taught me. I have my own two adorable kittens at my home in Fresno so we may have some issues if you're a dog lover, but I'm sure we will work it out. I still have my first American Sign Language pamphlets with basic signs, and if you're curious, I would love to practice with you. I'm an only child. My Dad passed away when I was 16, and my Mom is my everything. We have close family friends, the Coletts, who have practically adopted my Mom and me. They have been my supporters since I was born. I love them all dearly. If you hear me on a phone call, it is likely with one of them. You will probably see my Vihuela. I have played it for 5 years, and it makes me feel grounded in the music and refreshed by the energetic strumming patterns. Also, I keep a stack of my favorite movies in my room so we can pop a bag of popcorn and have a movie night! I look forward to our future adventures.

Dearly,

[NAME]

What is Meaningful to You?

This summer I had the opportunity to go outside my comfort zone with the Computer Science Logic Institute at Stanford. Since the program wasn't connected to my predominate academic interests, I decided to make this opportunity my own and reached out to professors on campus. One of them was the Deaf American Sign Language (ASL) professor. I was determined to meet her before the program finished so I had to think of another effective way to get in contact with her besides email. I approached one of the logic professors at the program, and they facilitated the connection the same day! We met at the Starbucks on campus and quickly bonded over Deaf rights and involvement in our respective ASL communities.

As I walked away from Starbucks I felt proud of my growth during the meeting. I was able to confidently network in my 3rd language with sufficient knowledge in the language and culture. I remember a period of time when I was too shy to speak up for what I wanted. I couldn't even ask for extra ketchup at McDonald's. This development would not have been possible if it weren't for the Ivy League Project where I learned how to network and be confident. Before I attended the Logic Institute, I was able to practice these skills on our visit to the Ivy League Universities. Thinking back to this moment encourages me to keep a growth mindset as I approach more challenges.

What is the most significant challenge that society faces today?

Finding common ground and maintaining a respectful dialogue. Citizens' Climate Lobby has shown me the importance of common ground when lobbying, and I have noticed how effective it makes communication. With this in mind I believe we could ease the political polarization that we see today.

How did you spend your last two summers?

Challenged myself with college courses and worked towards my AA in American Sign Language Studies.

Represented my Latino and youth community with Citizens' Climate Lobby when lobbying on Capitol Hill for climate action.

Earned a full scholarship and negotiated housing in Palo Alto to attend Stanford's Logic Institute.

What historical moment or event do you wish you could have witnessed?

My Dad was a 20 year old farm worker in the Central Valley during the National Farm Workers Association movement. Since my Dad's passing, I have wondered how activists like Cesar Chavez impacted his life and how it felt seeing Latinos nationally take a stand for their human rights.

What five words best describe you?

Activist, empathetic, networker, curious, adaptive

When the choice is yours, what do you read, listen to, or watch?

"Quotes for Nasty Women" is my go to book for words of motivation and wisdom.

While driving, I listen to motivational TedTalks or various styles of Latino music like Mariachi, Huapango, or Corridos.

Documentaries to learn about new cultures and the conditions of oppressed populations.

Name one thing you are looking forward to experiencing at Stanford.

As a future Latina leader I am looking forward to initiating a new American Sign Language Club, attending political lectures, expanding the current mariachi group, and engaging in challenging conversations to grow as an individual and learn from others.

Imagine you had an extra hour in the day—how would you spend that time?

For 15 minutes I would focus on four different tasks:

1) Learn how to play the harp.

2) Petition my school board for more efficient and sustainable recycling on campus

3) Learn about the culture and communication method of the Deaf-Blind

4) Teach my Mom American Sign Language.

Elaborate on EC/Work experience

My strong mother has been a house cleaner since she was 12 years old in Guatemala. When I was freshman in high school, I began to assist my Mom with cleaning houses depending on the availability of work and my school schedule. I used the earnings to help my Mom pay for the bills, groceries, or my school expenses. My books for community college cost me "a pretty penny", as my Dad would say, so this gives me the opportunity to buy my own books and relieve some financial pressure from my Mom. This experience brings me closer to my Mom, teaches me the value of having a strong work ethic, and learning to balance school and work.

Activities

1.	Fresno City College High School Enrichment Program
9, 10, 11, 12 Year 12 hr/wk 47 wk/yr	Since the summer of 2015 I have earned 61 college units
2.	ASL Club at Fresno City College
11, 12 Year, break 2 hr/wk	Our club's purpose is to promote communication in ASL on and off campus, educate about Deaf culture, and socialize with the local Deaf community.
3.	Jim Costa Liaison—Citizens' Climate Lobby (CCL)
11, 12 Year 3 hr/wk 30 wk/yr	CCL is an environmental policy interest group. Accomplishments: full scholarship to international conference, 2 resolution letters from city councils
4.	President—Roosevelt High School Mariachi Band

10, 11, 12	Our Mariachi is a band and community. As President I lead the group to ensure our band works together.
Year	
5 hr/wk 38 wk/hr	
5.	Roosevelt's Folkorico Advanced Group
10, 11, 12	Our high school has a folkorico group where we connect to our culture and community through dance.
Year	
5 hr/wk 38 wk/hr	

Reader 1

Eval—on the fence/leaning in.

She is taking many additional college classes and is Valedictorian. Her interests for social sciences is real as she speaks to her love for ASL.

Interviewer goes to bat and gives context to obsessions with ASL as Dad and Mom are Hard of Hearing.

[NAME] has an incredibly strong and compelling story of a student coming with much adversity, tenacity, and dedication to her education that is noteworthy.

FRPL
SPHH
M—none—laborer
F—AA—deceased

87% of students are FRPL

Only 20% 4 year

LBO—Ivy League Project

[NAME] does a great job of telling us who she is in her writing her cape is a summation of her life growing up in an abusive household as well as being translator for mom when they left the father. "I began to see my education as my power. Education became my resistance against the odds.

In her IVE—referee to interview

I am leaning all the way in the admit with [NAME] as I think she'll come here and quickly take advantage of all we have to offer.

Writing:

Cape—family context growing up abusive home

ECE—experience cleaning with mom

Support—REDACTED

Reader 2

[NAME] has dealt with things that most have not. Her determination and grit are palpable.

Her desire to take full advantage of her education with an understanding that others aren't as lucky is incredibly self reflective. She has AA

PolySci major also A+

She has worked alongside mom to earn money for herself and studies.

I strongly lean in.

Interview Comments

Interview:

Intellectual vitality: 1

Depth and commitment: 1

Character and self presentation: 1

[NAME] is a remarkable young woman who will quite simply make both Stanford and our world better. You're familiar with what she has accomplished but it's context that makes what's she's done and who she is all the more remarkable.

Her educational commitment started first with honoring her parents. What she is learning gives her the tools to do the work which she is passionate about.

One passion is the environment where she is deeply engaged.

Fresno City College at 8th grade HS grad and AA grad.

[NAME] is soft spoken, gentle, bright, engaging, and warm. She is a remarkably effective communicator and values these skills. She reported having only a few friends but I think that's a function of her commitments, her seriousness of purpose, and her maturity.

She reached out to two Stanford professors. This wasn't in any way about advantaging herself. It was about making connections.

[NAME] is self-effacing and indeed remarkably self less. I would guess she won't sell herself like other students so let me advocate. [NAME] may be the most remarkable HS student I have ever met.

Further context: parents from Guatemala and Hard of Hearing immigrants. She grew up in a house with violence and her father is now deceased.

Who [NAME] is and what she has accomplished is all the more remarkable given this context.

Reader 1 Scores	
Metric	**Score**
Test Rtg	5
HSR	2
Support	3
EC	3
SP-IV	3
Eval	2-

Reader 2 Scores	
Metric	**Score**
Test Rtg	5
HSR	2
Support	3
EC	3
SP-IV	3
Eval	2

The Story

An immensely courageous applicant who overcomes hardships with grace and pushes herself to excel.

The Evidence

This student combines her background, family situation, and personal motivations into a serious application that truly makes her stand out. Given her personal context, the story she offers the reader is truly inspirational—having grown up in an abusive environment and forced to face the death of her father, her character and her accomplishments are exceptionally remarkable.

One of her most notable achievements is the completion of an Associate's degree in American Sign Language—something few high schoolers have the time and motivation to complete. This is in addition to working with her mother, which goes to show just how serious and time-consuming her commitments must have been.

The Technique

The essays are as candid as can be, and her no-nonsense tone complements the theme of her application—everything application sounds honest and sincere. Unlike many applicants who purposefully "package" themselves to fit an identity they're not, this student tells the reader her story like it is. Her application is a narrative that serves more to inform than to impress, and it's all the more impressive for that very reason.

Her involvement with her school's Mariachi band and folklorico group are not discussed in her essays, so they don't add much to her application. Nevertheless, everything else about her background and character is stellar.

Takeaways

If you've experienced difficult circumstances, make sure to discuss them.

Highlight where you've been, and where you're going to be.

You don't need to join every club or win every award; it's the substance that counts.

Profile IV

California

Personal Essay

I teetered on tippy-toes in muddy pink shoes, arms flailing as I balanced precariously on hexagonal-shaped stones. Ever since I was a little girl, my sister and I have meticulously arranged tile shards in wet cement to craft stepping stones for my grandma's garden. I am like these vibrant creations, a mosaic of the eclectic, colorful tribe I call family.

Seemingly random pieces fit perfectly together. One grandma passionately collects owl figurines; the other throws famously festive parties. One grandpa has a Gandalf beard and hauls logs with a tractor; the other knows a little something about everything. My dad is an IT manager; my mom runs a design company. My ex-Google-executive uncle broke a world record skydiving through the stratosphere at 800 mph; my aunt heads a philanthropist foundation. Just as mosaics blend lustrous glass with bits of stone and shells, I am a product of the multifaceted personalities and perspectives that surround me.

At family dinners, there's a hodgepodge of lively topics from the Dining Philosophers Problem—a computer science problem illustrating synchronization issues in concurrent algorithm design—to plans for our S'mores Galore party. My explorations are endless because I'm encouraged to delve into anything that piques my interest.

As I foray into my fascinations, my mosaic becomes more intricate. My parents don't call me [NICKNAME] just because it's my last name— my intrinsic inquisitiveness spurs me to enthusiastically unearth the unknown. My family's diverse experiences and spirited nature challenge me to analyze varying opinions to define my own beliefs. As a journalist in search of perspectives, I've been caught in a lockdown at a juvenile detention center while pursuing a story about teen offenders, and surrounded by thousands of gun protesters at a March For Our Lives rally.

Nevertheless, my curious adventures go beyond journalism. Compression shirts powered by machine learning are just one of my budding business ideas. Others have ziplined 1500 feet above the rainforest; I did it upside-down. I'm relieved zombie apocalypses aren't real but scared that zombie ladybugs brainwashed by parasitic wasps are.

Perhaps unaligned with the finer arts, I'm sometimes quirky, most often casual, generally unpolished. I'm the playful 5'9" gangly girl dancing in the streets who shuns jeans and wears Santa socks in September. While my sister and her friends raved over my prom pictures, I tend to channel my grandpa's comfortable over-sized shirts and scuffed boots —what my sister calls the "grey-blob look."

Bits of spunk and sparkle add pop to my composition. Performing a rap about ducks to depict Holden's ambivalent mood swings in The Catcher In The Rye? That was me. My friends groan when I joke that finding inner peas would be pear-fection. Wanna taco 'bout it? If you receive one of my handcrafted "52 Reasons Why You're Amazing" card decks, you'll know exactly why you've inspired me.

My mosaic has a relaxed vibe that makes a statement. When my company, Jobscopia—a data-driven resource to expose teens to the job market—was selected by an entrepreneurial incubator, I pitched my idea before 70 prospective teammates. I was pleasantly surprised to see in my evaluations that my "chillness" and open-mindedness to others' ideas were draws for people to work with me.

Even with unrefined edges, I leave an impression. Scrolling through Mogul's "50 High Schoolers You Need To Know About" list, my name is nestled between a Netflix star and the youngest Olympic gold-medalist snowboarder. I feel like a rough sketch amid a gallery of masterpieces.

But that's because my mosaic isn't done yet.

I'm perfectly comfortable with being a work in progress. I'm enjoying the evolution of my character, passions, and style. In a society of manufactured identities where the outrageously sexy, high-flying people appear to reign, I'm the coalescing mosaic—fearlessly forging my path, piece by unassuming, colorful piece, toward completing the unique work of art that is me.

Intellectual Vitality

I was instantly captivated. As I opened up another article to edit and saw an array of red lines swooping under words and phrases, I knew I had found my partner-in-crime. Grammarly is a writing enhancement platform that does it all, from basic grammar errors to advanced suggestions on contextualized language. Boy, English is messy, but together, there's no stopping us.

Nope, it's not a squad of grammar wizards or English elves behind the screen, but something far more magical: *artificial intelligence.*

Like all good partners, Grammarly has learned to understand me; the kinds of punctuation I use, the style patterns within my writing, grammar suggestions that I ignore.

Likewise, I'm attracted to learn more about Grammarly's mysterious algorithms. Every now and then, I tease Grammarly, mischievously starting a sentence with "And." The intriguing nature of our relationship enchants us to mutually adapt to one another the more time we spend together.

As I get more cozy with Grammarly, I ponder the implications of panpsychism. My partner shows no emotion, which is strange to me, as I'm a rainbow of them. I realize Grammarly is not its best self without me.

I regularly question how our future together will unfold. Will we know each other so well that it knows my next move before I make it? Perhaps it will read my thoughts. As long as artificial intelligence wants to know all about me, I want to know all about it. Partners-in-crime, we're destined to have more exciting adventures together.

Roommate Essay

Hey Roomie!

Don't be alarmed. I'm secretly a ninja.

Nope, it's not a coincidence that I grew up falling on my head learning how to do backflips on my backyard trampoline or going to kickboxing classes alongside a bunch of middle-aged-tattooed dudes. Both were a part of my agility training. Sometimes, you'll catch me goofily dancing or belting my heart out to 2010 throwbacks but don't be fooled. My smiley persona is merely a ploy to distract you from my true identity.

You'll notice that my wardrobe is a collage of black, gray, and blue. I had to throw in two other colors just so people wouldn't be suspicious.

You'll never see me wearing jeans. Ever. They're obviously the worst fashion choice for a ninja.

Oh yeah, I'm really flexible. Most people can touch the tips of their fingers to their toes—I can touch my elbows to my toes. My stealth is also heightened by my sharp-as- cheddar-cheese eyesight (when my -4.75 contact lenses are in, of course).

Not to intimidate, I've thoroughly mastered the art-of-mind control. Whenever I sense someone feeling down, I get to work. Often I get crafty: a handmade sewn monster for my friend when his grandpa died or a midnight race down to my school armed with fresh cup-cakes and Netflix when my girlfriend's parents fought. After receiving my little gifts, they're usually feeling a little bit happier. Boom, mind control.

So now that I've shared mine, what's your secret identity?

Wa-choww ~[NAME]

What is Meaningful to You?

I think I might have a tab addiction.

Yup... 417 tabs on my MacBook may be just a little excessive. In spite of my friends' intervention, I cherish my beautifully cluttered culmi-nation of tabs.

My friends wonder if I know anything about bookmarks, and I do. But I'm reluctant to part with my tabs because they're a timeline of my re-cent past, a log of my thought processes, and a collection of disparate eye-opening ideas that have evolved my thinking.

One cluster reflects an obsession with Parisa Tabriz and her hacking highness, ethical of course. There was the time my mind exploded trying to fathom the complexities of a crumpled paper ball. TedTalks led me down a rabbit hole as I explored my Feminist label. Jeff Bezos is definitely taking over the world; I can prove it. The paradox of choice is truly a conundrum—is more really less?

Perhaps there is a breaking point to my organized chaos, but for now, I'm willing to suppress my subtle lurking fear that my laptop is about to catch on fire.

My tabs aren't just hoarded random curiosities. They are like hundreds of mirrors reflecting the bouncing thoughts in my brain—perspectives that have shaped my present-day character, innovations that are fueling my future, and visuals that are inspiring my creative expression. It is a meaningful comfort knowing that all these divergent ideas are accessible facets of me, still alive and well, just waiting to be spurred again.

What is the most significant challenge that society faces today?

The empathy crisis. We're becoming dangerously numb to the problems that plague those around us. Instead, we use the principle of self-preservation to rationalize a self-serving approach to global issues that require a one-world mindset. There is an "Us vs. Them" attitude that's silently mushrooming, building walls instead of bridges.

How did you spend your last two summers?

2017: Quarter Zero Entrepreneur Incubator—Chicago/NYC. Stanford Daily Journal Internship. Stanford PayPal research internship under Pamela Hinds. Perfecting malasadas & camping

2018: Girl Scout Camp counselor. Only HS Intern, Block Cypher. UC Berkeley Research Asst under Juliana Schroeder. Continued Stanford internship. Vacationed Oregon, Washington, Alaska. Gearing up for Editor-In-Chief :)

What historical moment or event do you wish you could have witnessed?

Hachiko, an Akita dog, waited nine years at a Tokyo train station for his owner's return after the man died unexpectedly at work. Remarkably, Hachiko demonstrated stronger values than most people who often quickly give up on one another. His unwavering devotion and patience are simultaneously extraordinary and heart-breaking.

What five words best describe you?

thankful, sponge, clumsy, playful, ready

When the choice is yours, what do you read, listen to, or watch?

Favorite journalism: *National Geographic*, *Time*, *NYT*. I absorb the blog *Wait But Why* & Quora. Creative muse: Pinterest. Binge-watched: Ted-Ed, *The Office*, *Orange is the New Black*. My nose is in these books: *Gang Leader For a Day*, *Freakonomics*, and the hilarious *Hyperbole and a Half*. Archie comics are my childhood.

Name one thing you are looking forward to experiencing at Stanford.

For years, I've led a team at the Green Library for a trivia hunt. I've spent hours running up and down West Stack's cream stairs, grazing my head on the low ceiling. I'm pumped to spend my Cardinal days there discovering dusty books with random knowledge at my finger-tips.

Imagine you had an extra hour in the day—how would you spend that time?

My kitchen is my playground. There's a deep satisfaction in being able to create dishes that evoke comfort, pleasure, and delight. It's pure exploration; just a few tweaks transforms a recipe into something entirely different. It's one of the places I can fail, make adjustments, and immediately try again.

Elaborate on EC/Work experience

Last year, I reached out to Professor Pamela Hinds within the Stanford Management and Sciences and Engineering Department, which landed me an opportunity to work alongside several enthusiastic graduate students on a research study that examined the effect of reflexivity on innovation.

PayPal's Head of Creativity wanted to find ways to make his multicultural work teams more innovative. My role entailed transcribing numerous videos of brainstorming sessions and categorizing every idea, identifying whether it was a new thought or related to an aforementioned concept. I was also tasked with summarizing the implications of each idea, which tested my understanding of the connected concepts.

The participants had very diverse lingual accents which made my job challenging. I enjoyed observing the animated collaboration and conceptualization of cutting-edge technologies on the verge of creation. The real-world innovations were compelling and I saw how team-building and self-reflection exercises can significantly change team dynamics.

Activities

1.	Member Girl Scouts of America
2nd grade—present 150 hr/yr	Counselor, Diamond Crest Camp. Volunteer & Food Distribution: Shelters, Churches, Ronald McDonald House. Bronze: Having Grit, Silver: Cancer Portrayed
2.	Member, Basketball Team
9, 10, 11, 12 13 hr/wk	On Freshman team was MVP and Captain Soph, Jr, Sr: Varsity Team. Qualified for CCS Selected to volunteer at Summer Camps (2), one for middle schoolers, one underrepresented elementary and middle school
3.	Intern, Stanford Center for Work Technology & Org.
11, 12 10-14 hr/wk	w/ Prof Pamela Hinds & Ph.D. H. Altman, researched Paypal innovation process; transcribed video & ideas, analyzed/developed reflexivity behavior codes
4.	Editor-In-Chief, Carlmont Journalism
10, 11, 12	National award Pacemaker 2017, developed multimedia program (8 projects); oversee 80 student writers

5.	Founder, Quarter Zero
10, 11 15-20 hrs/wk	Started my company idea Jobscopia as 1 of 10 Founders. Led team of 7 students
6.	Intern, BlockCypher
12 10 hrs/wk 3 wk/yr	Built cryptocurrency mining computers, each valued at >$10,000 for cryptocurrency startup; learned about backend mining software
7.	Member, The Junior Academy (New York Academy of Sciences)
10, 11 4 hr/wk 6 wk/yr	Online platform w/ elite-intl-STEM students. 13% acceptance. Grand Prize vs 350+ teams for Global Health Challenge (tracking Ebola survivors w/ tech)
8.	Lead Carlmont Ambassador
9, 10, 11, 12 30 hr/yr	Selected to represent Carlmont to incoming parents of potential students and Carlmont alumni; Take parents on tours of high school; answer questions in a panel
9.	Intern, Stanford Daily
11 6 hr/wk 10 wk/yr	Wrote articles published on the Stanford Daily's website. Attended Stanford Daily workshops. 1st ever high schooler published on U.S. Department of Energy site.
10.	Research Assistant, Berkeley
12 8 hr/wk	Worked under Prof J. Schroeder; observed & transcribed behavioral videos; how technology affects participant behavior, debating & pitching nonprofits

Reader 1

Well-rounded minus CS

PE: Nice essay that explores the "mosaic" of her personality and how it's made up of family and life experiences. Self-reflective comprehension

SQs: Stand strong

IV: Using tech for writing

RME: cute and clever

WM: about her tabs, creative and thoughtful

- description: reflective, creative, well-done

- mature voice, cleverly and creatively written

- interesting unique combined interest in writing and tech/AI, she has had a few internships where she was able to explore this.

- she would be a unique addition to the class. I am hoping she will emerge

- [NAME] is a talented writer as seen in her awards, publications, SQ writing, and PE

Reader 2

Went to 2 on EC because demonstrated excellence in journalism. Agree with R1, right on SPIV 2, stay at 3 though. Leaning in, but sending for a third reader for clarity.

Compelling for unique journalism and because PE was insightful and unique. Extended metaphor with mosaic making up personality—really nice PQs and signs of friendship.

RM: also unique (has a nice ending—"So what's your secret"), comparing to a ninja and actually manages to come together

Historical Moment: community member/friendship

IV: nice glimpses

WM: "My tabs aren't ... spurred again" (*quote from my essay*)

Friendship: "Bits of spunk ... inspired me" (*quote from my essay*)

Reader 3

[NAME]'s application was a fun read—her personality definitely comes through in all her responses, yet can be serious and thoughtful when needed.

It's an application you read and just want to invite her for a cup of coffee for conversation because you know you'll leave with it both having learned something but also have a smile on your face.

Her mature voice comes through clearly and creatively in writing

Her family has a nickname of [NICKNAME] for her. Her engagement and leadership are at 2-range for me as well. I actually see both readers on the same page and I stand there as well. Lots to like here and worth some time in committee.

Reader 1 Scores	
Metric	**Score**
Test Rtg	2
HSR	3
Support	3
EC	3
SP-IV	3
Eval	3+

Reader 2 Scores	
Metric	**Score**
Test Rtg	2
HSR	3
Support	2
EC	2
SP-IV	3
Eval	2-

The Story

An entrepreneurial student who is ready to use her pen to bring tech into society.

The Evidence

The major commitments which stand out to the readers are journalism and technology—and rightfully so. The applicant's spike is her writing—she's spent two summers interning for the Stanford Daily, as well as writing for her school newspaper, and many of her awards and honors are for her articles.

A great secondary pursuit is technology and entrepreneurship. She's interned at a company, and writes about how she's co-founded her own. Although there wasn't much elaboration or quantification of impact, the applicant does a great job integrating her interest in technology with writing, in her intellectual vitality essay, as well as the topic of her research activities.

Note that this applicant also had major commitments to basketball and Girl Scouts, but because they didn't fit the story, they didn't make it into the essays, and they didn't make it into the minds of the readers.

The Technique

This application has some very strong essays in it—in particular, the personal essay and roommate essay stood out in the minds of the readers. The third reader was almost entirely won over by her personality, demonstrated through her writing style. The essays are delightful because they're informal, well composed, focused, and each funny/unique—certainly an advantage of having such a deep background in journalism and writing.

This applicant has the unique advantage of demonstrating an incredibly strong commitment to Stanford—interning at the Stanford Daily and doing research with faculty here for two years. Don't be disheartened; the admissions officers didn't mention it at all. However, this commitment helped in a different way—the applicant knew what tone to write in, and what activities and groups she's excited to be a part of.

Takeaways

Admissions officers note creative writing.

If essay tidbits are funny or unique, they'll be remembered.

Commitment to a specific university is great, if only because you've implicitly done the research.

Profile V

Hawaii

Personal Essay

The light shines so brightly in my face I can barely see, but still, I walk forward. My arms feel hot with anticipation, itching to break out from my grasp. Even though I am blinded momentarily, I stride forward with confidence; I trust the path on which I walk on. At last, my destination approaches, and the light finally eases. My friend stands beside me as we both grip our bows in excitement for what lies ahead. We sit down together and place our violas on our shoulders, ready to release the sumptuous melodic genius of Elgar. The concert is about to begin, 105 of us watch in anticipation as the baton drops and cues the dawn of symphony.

In music, competition greets you from any and all directions, whether it be symphonic performance or composition. Yet, there's an element of unified purpose that can be found within it, especially in the symphony. Despite being separated into different instrument families and ranked from 1st chair to last, the purpose of each player remains consistent.

I am only one musician, with only one instrument, and one seat. My sound is insignificant compared to the grand orchestra. But I am a part of it, I contribute to it, and I share a place on the stage with many other musicians, who also, have one instrument, and one seat. We unite to create music, and that purpose binds us into a collective orchestra.

However, there is a deeper desire that I personally have when performing, much more profound than the symphony itself. I play my music for that moment when my body is seconds away from giving up on me; my face is drenched in sweat, and as I lift my bow off the string for the last note, I look back into the audience. There is a second of silence, where nothing in the room moves, as if time stopped, and we all revel together in the glory of the music. In this moment, I am joined with everyone in the auditorium under one common task: listening. The impact of the symphony isn't just being united to create music, but to unite while creating music.

I discovered later in my life that these moments of silence do not only occur when I play music. When I shoot archery, I go through a few similar seconds of silence, when I am lost in sheer concentration, and all sound around me stops. Then, when the moment is just right, I release. Even in this moment, everything feels connected; my bow and my body are one, unified to achieve this task. I believe there are experiences like this in everything we do, we just need to discover them, like I did when I played the final note of Elgar's Finale.

And so, it is my purpose to play music. It is in my hope that one day, the entire world, perhaps even the universe, can have that second of silence after the symphony performs. A moment where we can all bond in a sense of unanimity so beautiful that even if temporary is worth dedicating your life toward.

Intellectual Vitality

When I get to apply my creative side into a lesson, I get to deepen my understanding of a concept. Usually, it's easier to explore that outside of the classroom because I can discover different ideas and ways to express them through my own artistic methods. Inside the classroom, there tends to be restrictions on creative expression in assignments; however, when it is allowed, I like to make rap verses based on the lesson and share them during presentations. Rhyming "Psittaciformes" with "tax reforms" in a taxonomy song is much more memorable than blandly stating it in a powerpoint slide. It makes it fun not only for myself, but for my peers and teacher too.

Roommate Essay

Aloha,

My name is [NAME]. I'm very excited to share the Stanford experience with you and the extremely welcoming community here. Even if we are in different classes, there are numerous opportunities to learn beyond the classroom and I hope that we can go on this adventure together. I've never had a roommate before so always feel free to let me know if there are any inconveniences or poor habits that I bring to the room. We are both human, with our own needs, and I am completely prepared to do my best to meet yours. I may not always be able to assist with your studies, but I can always provide emotional support. I make incredible Spotify playlists for just about any situation. Sometimes I just sit down and play the piano to make people feel good. I even take song requests—give it a day or two and I'll play it for you. Aside from my music, I love to play team based video games (when I have the time to, of course) and shoot archery. But enough about me, tell me about yourself and your interests. I can't wait to meet you in person and learn about your journey to the Stanford campus.

From,

[NAME], your roommate

What is Meaningful to You?

My ears are easily my most valuable tools. To me, there is no life or meaning to anything without sound. Even when I internally read a word, I revel in its beautiful and particular musicality as it forms its own symphonic sentence. I listen to my surrounding environment to help me understand the world I stand on. I listen to silence to reflect on myself and cherish the tranquility of this precious moment. Most importantly, however, I listen to people to understand the world they live in. Each person has their own story, their own message they have to share, but it doesn't mean anything if they aren't heard. I make it my responsibility to pay attention to the fascinating melody of each person's story.

What is the most significant challenge that society faces today?

The discrimination of those who identify as LGBTQ. Genuine tolerance is advocated across the world, as is evident through the decline of racism, and yet, society still finds it hard to value and recognize those for the people they love.

How did you spend your last two summers?

I took on different challenges, two of the most significant ones being archery and entering a piano competition. Both processes helped me become more confident in myself and realize that while there may be some areas I excel in, they shouldn't be the only things I do.

What historical moment or event do you wish you could have witnessed?

I would want to witness any moment before the Industrial Revolution, when air pollution did not exist to the degree it does today, and humans could see the stars from their backyard.

What five words best describe you?

Learn to lead by listening

When the choice is yours, what do you read, listen to, or watch?

Being on a small island, attending Hawaii Symphony Orchestra's concerts is easily accessible and something I take advantage of regularly. When I listen, I hear no difference between them and the New York Philharmonic. To me their sound is equally beautiful, yet they are not on the same level of prestige.

Name one thing you are looking forward to experiencing at Stanford.

When I visited Stanford over the summer, I received an immense impression of unity and teamwork. Many college environments are very competitive and students fight to be better than their classmates. I want to work with my peers and not just try to get the highest GPA among them.

Imagine you had an extra hour in the day—how would you spend that time?

I write music, primarily song remixes, to share my interpretation of the story behind them. Each person listens to the same song, but each story behind that person is very different. I want to share the ideas that I have with everyone, and the creative ways I can convey them.

Elaborate on EC/Work experience

I talk a great deal about my musical background because it is definitely a source of great pride; however, there is a new side of me I recently discovered. Last summer, I applied for a job at my school to be a leader at at a summer fun program. I wanted work experience, but dreaded the idea of working with children, especially the little ones that were barely potty trained. However, to my surprise, I immediately warmed up to them, and even continue to work part time at the after school care program held during the school year. Taking part in this field of work also gave me tools to become a better leader; after all, if I had the ability to direct one hundred kids, I could definitely lead a class council meeting.

Activities

1. Music: Instrumental	Hawaii Youth Symphony
9, 10, 11, 12 School 3 hr/wk, 43 wk/yr Continue	2016: Featured on NPRs, From the Top. 2017-2019: Collaborated with the Hawaii Symphony Orchestra for two concerts.
2. Athletics: Club	Archery, 50th State Archery Club
10, 11, 12 Year 5 hr/wk, 50 wk/yr	2016-2018: Trained in the Olympic Style Recurve Bow. 2017: Received 2nd place in the state for age group.
3. Science/Math	Oahu Math League
10, 11, 12 School 1 hr/wk, 40 wk/yr	Practiced various areas of math for monthly meets. 2018: Achieved highest scorer in school for one meet.
4. Theater/Drama	IPA Theatre Department/Sound Engineer
10, 11, 12 School 8 hr/wk, 24 wk/yr Continue	Put on 2 productions per year: 1 play and 1 musical. I led the sound engineering crew and ensured quality sound during the shows.
5. Academic	IPA Japanese National Honor Society/ JNHS President
11, 12 School 2 hr/wk, 35 wk/yr Continue	Recognizes students who show a passion for the Japanese language and culture. I organize meetings, cultural events, induction ceremony

6. Academic	IPA National Honor Society
11, 12 School 2 hr/wk, 35 wk/yr Continue	Recognizes students who demonstrate 4 pillars: Scholarship, Leadership, Service, Character. I organized and helped lead service projects
7. Music: Instrumental	IPA Mixing Club/Mixing Club President and Founder
12 School 1 hr/wk, 40 wk/yr Continue	Taught high school kids who are interested how to produce music digitally on computer using DAW Software. I organized meetings and online competitions
8. Community Service (Volunteer)	IPA Mu Alpha Theta/Math Honor Society Secretary
11, 12 School 1 hr/wk, 35 wk/yr Continue	Tutor math students of any grade level during study hall periods. During meetings, I record the minutes and print the agenda
9. Work (Paid)	IPA After School Care/Assistant Teacher
12 School 4 hr/wk, 40 wk/yr Continue	Supervised kindergarten kids after school. Organized games, activities, and lessons for them to do until they were picked up by guardians.
10. Athletics: Club	Other Sport, IPA Ultimate Club
11, 12 Year 2 hr/wk, 45 wk/yr Continue	Trained in fundamentals of Ultimate. Taught newcomers how to throw a disc, organized a friendly annual tournament with other schools

INSIDE STANFORD ADMISSIONS

Reader 1

ERW: 740

MS: 770

ES-W: 16

MW: Popcorn responses are especially thoughtful, gem of essay is MW.

Reader 2

HSR: Definitely a MD

Reader 1 Scores	
Metric	**Score**
Test Rtg	2
HSR	3
Support	2
EC	3
SP-IV	2
Eval	2

Reader 2 Scores	
Metric	**Score**
Test Rtg	2
HSR	3
Support	2
EC	2
SP-IV	3
Eval	

The Story

A viola maestro, engaged in society.

The Evidence

There is an overwhelming amount of emphasis on the applicant's musical involvement: five essays, two activities, awards, and a musical supplement. The spike in this application is certainly the viola.

At the same time, there's some evidence for the care the applicant has for imparting knowledge—two activities about teaching. There are also secondary involvements in archery, theatre, math, and NHS, but these are not developed in any essays.

The Technique

There's a clear passion for music, and a clever bridge to social activism and tolerance. The applicant talks about the "fascinating melody of each person's story" in his what is meaningful essay, which was commented on by the readers. His five words and "Most Important Problem" essay show similar dedication to inclusivity. There are, of course, disjoint or unconnected pursuits—archery, math, and after-school care, but these don't detract from the major thrust of the application.

Takeaways

Interesting writing can push you over the line.

Having a clear message that aligns with your spike can make up for a weaker profile.

Essay Sets

Finally, here's the meat-and-bones: Sets of Stanford college application essays, along with the real comments and numerical ratings that Stanford gave to each applicant. We've organized these submissions into three categories: Against All Odds, Academic Powerhouses, and Cultural Catalysts.

Against All Odds

Profile I

Kenya

Personal Essay

I was eleven when I started to question my sexuality.

I was scared, a preteen African girl who saw being gay as what it had always been portrayed to be—illegal, against God and against her culture. In my community, girls are married off by the time they are sixteen so when I was thirteen, talks of a suitor began. I was worried, I loved being in school and getting married would disrupt any chances I had of completing my education. There was also the fact that I wasn't attracted to the suitors. In the midst of my confusion, I decided to talk to someone. I came out to my favorite uncle and he raped me on three different occasions claiming I was yet to experience what a man had to offer. He would slap me and spit on me in the name of conversion therapy. I was scared to live in my own house. I decided to report the case at the local police station and it was thrown out because the officer-in-charge was homophobic. Eventually my uncle moved out, but the memories remained.

I felt alone and confused. I felt dirty, but I could not talk to anyone for fear of outing myself. My feelings soon morphed into anger. I was angry that society valued saving a man's face over a girl's pain. I was angry that my sexuality was enough reason to label me as invalid and that all society would ever see me as is my husband's trophy.

By the end of 2013 my parents had found a suitor. I began panicking. I had just done my KCPE exams and was the first girl from my constituency to ever get above 400 marks out of 500. I wanted to go to high school. I spent numerous nights pleading with my parents. Mother agreed but Father remained rigid. I decided to go to the County Education Officer and requested him to persuade Father. That night, Father beat me for airing out our problems. That was not the first time he beat me. He would come home drunk and beat all of us, including Mother. That night however, was the last. Mother took my brothers and I and we fled, never to see Father again.

I was set to start high school in January.

During my first year in high school, I came out to my then best friend and told her what happened with my uncle, and she spread the news like wildfire. I was constantly mocked for being queer and some even said that the rape was my fault. This made me regret insisting on joining high school. In Form Two, Stephanie (an alumna of my high school) came to talk to us. She discussed overcoming challenges similar to mine, excelling in KCSE, and going to study in a top U.S. university. After the talk, I went and confided in her and she offered to mentor me. She reminded me that I was not a mistake and my that successes would inspire other girls and queer teenagers. Soon enough I was top of my class, chair of two clubs, and participating in various competitions. I had finally earned my classmates' respect. I believe my resilience and determination are why I was elected as the school captain. I passed KCSE and became the first girl from my village to qualify to join university.

I did not forget my resolve to help empower girls and thus in October, I volunteered at Moringa School; teaching young girls coding and mentoring them to believe that despite what society dictated, they were not inferior to men. Moreover, I joined the Gay and Lesbian Coalition of Kenya (GALCK) as a peer counselor; supporting queer teens in their journey to self-discovery.

My journey is far from over, but I am also far from giving up.

A luta continua

The struggle continues.

Intellectual Vitality

As her casket was lowered into the ground, a sense of responsibility rose in me. I needed to do something.

This was the second time in six months that my village had been hit by flash floods. As a fourteen year old, the idea of death seemed extremely abstract until I encountered it first hand. My cousin Awino had been by the river when the floods hit. Her body was found six kilometers away from the village. The pain of losing a close cousin and friend motivated me to begin research on how disasters like those could be better managed.

It was during my research that I discovered that the solution to such a big problem lay between my fingers and a keyboard. I saw an article discussing an application in France that warned citizens of ongoing forest fires and linking them to emergency services. I soon realized that a similar program could be developed for floods, and I could improve on it by warning the users on which days flooding is likely to occur, and linking the users to each other so that they can share their locations when floods hit.

Through majoring in Computer Science and learning how to develop the system as well as other programs that will help to avert danger and save lives during crises, I would have finally found a way to honor Awino.

Roommate Essay

Jambo!

Congratulations on getting into Stanford. I honestly can't wait to meet you!

First, let me warn you. Depending on who you ask, I may or may not snore a lot. I really don't like making my bed and I listen to Bohemian Rhapsody more times than a normal human should. I love African music, so you may have to bear with listening to Afropop for a couple of minutes each day.

I hope none of these will be a deal breaker to you. I can't wait to find out what your quirks are (I am silently hoping that one of them is that you enjoy making beds). I'm sure we'll be quick friends. I can only imagine how much I have to learn from you. Just the thought of it gets me excited.

I have so much to share with you; from photos of my homeland to Swahili phrases to Kenyan dance styles such as Bazokizo. I love cooking. Hopefully you'll try out some of my chapatis. Keep in mind that I said I love cooking, not that I'm particularly good at it.

A new chapter of our lives is about to begin and I am very grateful for the chance to experience it with you.See you on campus and Go Cardinals!

With love,
Your roommate [NAME].

What is Meaningful to You?

I stood up and gave him a hug.

"[NAME] I can't do this anymore. My parents hate me… everybody hates me." Kamau sobbed into my shoulder

Working with the Gay and Lesbian Coalition of Kenya has been emotional. Everyday I see teenagers suffer because of who they chose to love. Susan's parents shaved off all her hair when she came out to as bisexual, Wanyama, transgender, was beaten to a pulp by his (now her) brother and Njambi, a lesbian, was taken before a local church every Sunday for 2 months so that the members could exorcise the "demon of homosexuality" from her. All of them were eventually banished from their homes.

Despite the fact that at GaLCK we link these teenagers to hospitals and to allies in the police force, their cases almost never make it to court. Reassuring queer teens that their hearts are not wrong healed wounds in my heart that I didn't even know

172

I had. Seeing them, 12—16 year olds, looking so dejected and beaten up, with broken bones and broken hearts, having no homes to go to and nowhere to run to within our government (because in Kenya being queer is illegal) left me angered by our system.

I believe that everyone has their opinions, but no one's opinion should be a reason to deny someone else their rights. I want to change this.

I will change this, one step at a time.

That is why for now, I will keep reassuring Kamau.

What is the most significant challenge that society faces today?

Despite the growing importance of the internet in today's world, only about 14% of Africans are connected to the internet. From cloud services, connecting producers to their market, enhancing education, breaking communication barriers, and easier access to social services; connectivity to the internet is the solution Kenya, and Africa, needs.

How did you spend your last two summers?

2017: Other than studying for K.C.S.E, I visited my grandparents and looked after my sick grandfather together with taking online classes in Python.

2018: Between volunteering at Moringa, playing a few concerts, and working as a teaching assistant in Kerarapon primary, my time slots were packed.

What historical moment or event do you wish you could have witnessed?

I wish I was there in 1952 when Grace Hopper invented CO-BOL, the first ever programming language to use words instead of numbers in code. I would like to witness the steps she took to develop this revolutionary language that was well ahead of its time

What five words best describe you?

Spectacles, keyboard, questions, inventions, solutions

When the choice is yours, what do you read, listen to, or watch?

My dad always played Lucky Dube's music in the house. I still remember dancing with him to " Ding Ding Licky Licky Licky Bong". Despite all the pain he caused, those carefree moments always come to mind when I think of him.

On my playlist, Dube is always on repeat.

Name one thing you are looking forward to experiencing at Stanford.

Whether it's in the Stanford Information Networks Group (SING), the Wireless Sensor Networks Laboratory, or even helping in research, I would exploit the chance to learn under Philip Levis—through whom I will gain invaluable information on networking and sensor technology, key areas in development of disaster management systems.

Imagine you had an extra hour in the day—how would you spend that time?

I usually focus more on the trees rather than the forest. Given an extra hour, I would allow myself to zoom out and focus less on software, and more on the machine. I would love to engage in the building and wiring of robots, rather than programming ready made parts.

Reader 1

Her strength comes from non cogs—grit and her strength of educational commitment paired with her engagement in CS. Strong sense of self comes through as well. Has overcome so much, seeks to help others, excels academically and in her field of study. Strong inclination to community service.

Reader 2

Excellent academic record, clear impact in ECs. Non- cog strengths abound. Distance travelled us a POE. Resilience is one of her strengths and POE. EC's show leadership particularly in CS.

Tags

GEN1

Reader 1 Scores	
Metric	**Score**
Test Rtg	3+
HSR	3+
Support	2+
EC	2+
SP-IV	2+
Eval	2+

Reader 2 Scores	
Metric	**Score**
Test Rtg	2
HSR	2-
Support	2+
EC	2+
SP-IV	2+
Eval	2+

Profile II

Kansas

Personal Essay

In my childhood, I nearly drowned—twice. I was scared to death. I did not know how to swim. I remember the water filling my lungs, screaming and kicking, desperately trying anything to get my head above the surface. Looking back, I laugh. I laugh at the naive little girl, asking her "Why were you so terrified of drowning when you had so many people around who could rescue you?"

Later that year, my family could not afford our apartment and we were forced to move in with my grandparents. I remember one night, clear as water, I sat at the dining room table with my grandpa and dad working on my homework. I was focused on my long division problems when my dad suddenly turned to me. I was taken aback when my dad told me he loved me, but he also brought up our circumstances, trying to explain our situation. I tightened my grip on my pencil, my heart squeezing. "[NAME], this is all my fault, I didn't work hard enough for myself or our family. I've made too many mistakes and I don't want you making them either." I looked at my dad, who looked so resentful and sorry for his decisions and how they affected our family. Right then and there, I made a promise to myself: I would work my hardest in school to make my family proud and myself stable, successful, and most importantly, happy with my life.

After becoming so determined, I strove to build up my academic resume as well as the activities I was involved in. Just one dilemma: I had no idea what I was doing. Wading into the sea of confusion that is middle and high school, I must have looked like a fish out of water frantically searching for opportunities. With immense pressure to excel and having such high expectations of myself, I almost drowned a third time.

I was overwhelmed. I felt like I had stones in my pockets. Thankfully, my friends noticed my struggle. As a person who is reluctant to ask for help especially when I need it most, it was not easy to share my problems and burdens with them. At the time, I was ashamed of sharing my personal struggles, but now I am eternally grateful I did.

Knowing what I was going through, my friends helped me shape my goals for success and the path I would take to get there. By going to volunteer events with me, telling me what prep books to get, which AP classes were worth taking, inviting me to study groups, and even suggesting the most relaxing focus playlists on Spotify, my friends were my life jacket; they helped me keep my head above water.

Now that I had a support system, it was much easier to approach the adults in my life with specific questions about my future. Since neither of my parents went to college and have little experience with the path to get there, I only relied on them for moral support. That being said, entering high school, I did not have an adult to go to with my neverending college questions; well, that is until I joined student government. I was able to grow closer to my sponsor, Ms. Derks, connecting immediately with how passionate she always was about the things she did. I went to her whenever I was struggling, and she always provided me with the advice and support I needed. While my friends helped keep me afloat, I was always just simply treading water. Ms. Derks taught me how to swim.

In the beginning, I was so focused on my own confusion that I was oblivious to the many people in my life willing to help me. Truthfully, I may have always been stubbornly independent, but allowing myself to ask for help and be vulnerable was the best thing I could have ever done. My friends and Ms. Derks were my lifeline; they kept me from drowning. They guided me in my journey of becoming my own person, fueling my passions, motivation, and determination to become the strong-willed girl I am today and the successful woman I want to be.

Intellectual Vitality

Sitting in my freshman Honors Biology class, notebook and highlighters neatly organized on my lab table—this is where I fell in love. No, not with a person, but a carcinogenic concept. It may be alarming for some to think about it, a fifteen-year-old girl infatuated with oncology; however, it was an inspiration for me. At this very point in my life, I began to know why I was working so hard in school, why I wanted so desperately to help others. Just the idea of studying, diving deeper into such a field excited me to no end. I could not wait to specialize in this medical profession, anxiously awaiting graduation and college even though I had not yet begun to experience high school. Well, that is until it happened.

At the end of my freshman year, I found out my grandfather had a brain tumor. His death shattered me, and the fact that those little malignant cells were the cause just irked me. If I did not want to change the future of medicine more before, I definitely did now. I never wanted anyone else to experience the pain and loss I felt, the one my best friend felt when her dad passed away from prostate cancer, like what any victim of cancer's family felt. No, I wanted and still want families to celebrate and cry tears of joy when their loved one survives, is cured and cancer free. I want to change the face of cancer research and treatment.

Roommate Essay

Hi! There is a lot to know about [NAME]!

Firstly, although I can be very outgoing, seeking adventure and opportunity often, I am very much a homebody and an introvert. I like having my own personal space, but if you want to stay in and watch a movie six out of seven nights during the week, just hanging out, I am here to be your official couch buddy.

Next, I need to just outright say it: I am a complete night owl. I hate mornings with a burning passion but I can pull an all nighter, staying up until 4am without a problem. If you too are a night person, we will get along well.

Continuing, I am a music junky. I love almost all genres, except for country and metal. Nothing against them, I just personally do not like them, all except for Carrie Underwood's "Before He Cheats," I can sing my heart out to that song. Anyway, you will most likely see me carrying around my earbuds or headphones twenty-five hours a day, eight days a week; and do not worry, I have a speaker, too, so we can have all of the jam sessions you want.

Lastly, I would say I am quite a quirky person, as I have been told I have a 4D personality. I love making dad jokes, watching the most random of Youtube videos, and sparking the most peculiar conversations. Suffice to say, we will not have a boring first year together.

What is Meaningful to You?

One of the very basic keys to my personal being is music. I love and appreciate the wide variety of genres music contains. Pop would not be pop without R&B, R&B would not be R&B without rock, rock would not be rock without classical, and so on. Although music is always changing, artists innovating and pushing new music into the world, it has always been a constant in my life. There is never a single place I go without my earbuds; it is as if they are another appendage, perhaps even a vital organ. Music is the first thing I hear in the morning from my alarm, it is what I use to get through the day, what soothes my mind before bed. Whether it be teaching myself on my mini keyboard or putting on my headphones to tune out the noise of society, music is what seems to keep me alive and going.

I love understanding others through their taste in music; even by simply looking at a person's Spotify playlist, one can see how diverse and complex that individual is. I believe music is an outlet for people, a way to cope, to be happy, to cry, to relax, and simply a way for someone to express their thoughts and emotions. The connection music makes between people, building a bridge, even a foundation of understanding, is what draws me to it, makes it a part of me.

What is the most significant challenge that society faces today?

Today, meme culture is the world's most impending problem. No one knows if it is a joke anymore, there are too many trolls online, and we just cannot escape Kermit. Please listen and take this PSA to heart as we need to resolve the damage done by meme lords.

How did you spend your last two summers?

During my last two summers, I worked at a children's farmstead for most of my time off. It allowed me to learn patience and better social skills. Along with this, this past summer I attended a medical camp called Camp Cardiac, learning about the anatomy and physiology of the heart.

What historical moment or event do you wish you could have witnessed?

I would have loved to attend Woodstock. Simply being present at one of the best music festivals of all time would have been extraordinary and incredibly fun. Now we have Coachella, so maybe it could be a second chance for me.

What five words best describe you?

Determined, independent, optimistic, calm, outgoing

When the choice is yours, what do you read, listen to, or watch?

When I have free time, which is quite rare, I love to sit down and read a good dystopian or romance novel. I also love listening to kpop; reading and connecting with the lyrics of artists halfway across the world has always amazed and excited me.

Name one thing you are looking forward to experiencing at Stanford.

I am very excited to be surrounded by such driven, successful people. I believe I become more determined and motivated seeing individuals who are so passionate about something they love and believe in. With such diversity at Stanford, this will be easy to find for me.

Imagine you had an extra hour in the day—how would you spend that time?

Quite honestly, I would use the time to relax or sleep. I already do so much between school, extracurriculars, and work; I think a good mental health hour would be in store for me.

Reader 1

EC: impressive motivation working 20 hrs/week PTJ on top of family obligations and buy own meals, along with campus leadership, and IV in biology, stuco, frosh mentor, relay for life, volleyball, medical club, spanish national honor society, and math national honor society

SPIV: meet hist fig++, interdisciplinary interests (see fav subj), community member

QB 1: learn when and how to ask for help -well done

QB2: oncology -well done

IVE: same as QB 2

Tags

DIV, GEN1, QBF, QBM

Reader 1 Scores	
Metric	**Score**
Test Rtg	3
HSR	3
Support	3
EC	1
SP-IV	2
Eval	2

Profile III

New Hampshire

Personal Essay

I first experienced the power of prayer when I was thirteen. My family was sitting in our usual spot at church: the back row, where my autistic sister wouldn't cause too much of a disturbance if she had a meltdown. At the end of the service, a song began to play, and my mother kneeled at the foot of the stage with her mouth moving in a prayer inaudible from where I sat. Her eyes were closed, but I could tell she was crying from her trembling, reddening face.

I don't remember why my mother cried during that prayer. It could've been that our house was being foreclosed. Or it was that my sister Jen, who has severe autism, needed speech therapy we couldn't afford. Maybe it was that my oldest sister, Monica, could only apply to one local college because we needed her at home to help Jen. Or it was that my grandparents were getting older and more jaded from supporting my mother. Maybe it was that my father left her with four kids and no money. My mother never voiced these problems to us, only revealing them in her prayers or the hushed phone calls with her sister as I eavesdropped.

Since middle school, I hid my family life from my friends, inadvertently creating a different identity that I carried to Phillips Exeter Academy, a boarding school in New Hampshire. I never revealed that I was a financial aid student with one parent and an autistic sister – not out of shame, but because I couldn't find my voice. Then, in an English class, I found another outlet: writing. Finally, I began to tell my family's story.

I'm the youngest in a family of five: two sisters, one brother, one mother, and myself. After my father left when I was eight years old, my family struggled to compensate for his absence and care for Jen. I grew up helping Jen, seven years my senior, in brushing her teeth, using the restroom, making food for her, and helping her speak. While these experiences taught me independence, they also taught me about compassion for others. Jen doesn't have the privilege to interact and live as easily as I do. After I left for boarding school and my siblings for college, I noticed that Jen consequently regressed. During the summer of 2017, my mother and Jen moved from Connecticut to New Hampshire so that I could take care of Jen after classes on Wednesdays and the weekends.

My loyalty to Jen has meant sacrifices, but I'm also more appreciative of every opportunity. In 2017, I attended the Paideia Institute's month-long summer Latin program in Italy on two scholarships. More thankful for the opportunity, I cherished speaking Latin at the Circus Maximus and reading Latin inscriptions on the bridges in Rome. I also treasure attending the National Junior Classical League Convention every summer to represent New Hampshire at the national level. I value these experiences as rare gifts since I don't have the same opportunities as most students.

Through my hardships and accomplishments, I've relied on prayer and writing to guide me. At Phillips Exeter, I used my essays as outlets to reflect on my relationships with Jen and my family. Often, I find myself handwriting my prayers, expressing gratitude for my opportunities and praying for Jen to learn to speak. By finding an outlet for my feelings and leaning on prayer, I learned to address my past, cherish the present, and have faith for the future.

Watching my mother in church that day made me realize why prayer is so powerful. The broken and desperate rely on the sense-making and meaning that it provides. This sense-making is what drives my family to continue without my father. This meaning is what doesn't let us give up on Jen. This is what the power of prayer is for my family and me.

Intellectual Vitality

This April, I gathered the courage to email Dr. Andrew Zissos, Chair of the Department of Classics at UC Irvine. I didn't expect a response. A different professor had already turned me down the year before, but I didn't want to give up easily. I wanted to experience the real academic work outside my high school curriculum.

When I began in June, Dr. Zissos told me about the college textbooks he's been developing for undergraduate students and his work on the Society for Classical Studies' Latin and Greek Translation Database, aimed at making translations of ancient texts online and accessible to the public. I could work on one or both. How could I not choose both? For the textbooks, I chose Petronius' Satyricon and Book III of Julius Caesar's Bellum Civile. For the online database, I focused on compiling data for

Petronius' Satyricon, searching libraries for all online and physical translations of Petronius' Satyricon in multiple languages.

Through this experience, I progressed from learning Classics as a student to engaging as a contributor. No longer was I studying commentaries and answering questions from a textbook; I was creating them. Stepping into the role of a teacher made learning more exciting, because I knew I wasn't learning just for myself. In class, new thoughts engaged me, "How would I phrase a question about this construction? How can I help someone easily understand this author's tone?" After this summer, I found a greater need to learn more, so I could contribute more.

Roommate Essay

Dear Roommate,

Hello! I can't wait to meet you! Before I say anything else, you should know that I wholeheartedly believe in The Five Love Languages, a book which states that people give love in the way they want to receive love, and that understanding a loved one's unique love language can improve your relationship. Frankly, I've only read the Wikipedia page, but I employ the concept in my daily life. My love language is acts of service. I show my appreciation for my friends by making their lives easier such as getting them breakfast or making sure they've woken up for school on time. What's your love language?

I also make bucket lists when I visit new places. While making these lists has encouraged me to be adventurous, I've also learned to be patient when things don't go as planned.

Sometimes, I can't cross everything off (I still have yet to visit the Mark Twain House & Museum) but I'm a big believer of "It'll happen when it happens." So, Roommate, what would you put on your list?

My Stanford bucket list so far:

1. Play water polo again (had to quit because of a concussion, but it'll take more than that to stop me!)

2. Learn how to surf and join the surf club (embarrassing, I grew up in SoCal and should have learned already)

3. Master juggling (I've tried so hard, and if anybody's smart enough to teach me, it's Stanford students, right?)

What is Meaningful to You?

Many people are named after relatives or symbolic words. I, however, was named after my brother, [NAME], who's four years older than me. Growing up, I carried our shared name proudly and tagged along wherever he went.

[NAME] first encouraged me to play golf when I was six. Initially, we ran around swinging toy clubs. Then, we started competing, and I ranked 15th internationally at eight years old. We did Taekwondo together, and I became a black belt and national gold medalist at age eight. When [NAME] started water polo, I joined, competing in the Junior Olympics until my sophomore year and placing 9th when I was thirteen. We made practice exciting by creating new competitions and goals everyday, and my achievements and love for these sports developed from the fun.

I then found my passion for Classics after [NAME] introduced me to Latin. Although it never excited him, I found myself studying in Rome, competing in Certamen (Latin quizbowl) at the national level, and representing New Hampshire at the National Junior Classical League Convention every summer. I found something I wanted to explore, even if it was without [NAME].

Some believe that a person's name and its meaning can influence their life's trajectory. Whether that's true or not, I'm grateful [NAME] helped me find the things I love, yet there are more things to discover on my own. My name has become a message to be thankful for those who've guided me but to also make my own path.

What is the most significant challenge that society faces today?

It's someone at the airport calling a woman wearing a hijab "a terrorist" or a stranger screaming at my autistic sister for freezing up in a crowded place and blocking their way. We need to open our minds to others' experiences and struggles so that we can better understand them.

How did you spend your last two summers?

Learning Korean through a book borrowed from my Latin teacher, Latin-ing, hanging with Jen, trying to juggle (#3 on bucket list, you'll see later), praying, golfing, showing friends the wonders of Orange County's Little Saigon (Little Saigon is like a geode; it seems modest until you peek inside, please visit!)

What historical moment or event do you wish you could have witnessed?

[NAME] and I stationed ourselves around the tree. We placed wire around all entrances, and each of us drank three cups of hot chocolate to sustain us for the night. Santa Claus was ours … but somehow we still fell asleep.

That crafty, old man eluded us that night. I want answers.

What five words best describe you?

Female reincarnation of Julius Caesar

When the choice is yours, what do you read, listen to, or watch?

Watch: International television shows and movies, because it's interesting to learn about different cultures (fun fact, some schools in China have hot water fountains rather than cold ones)

Listen: BTS, online sermons

Read: Funny Amazon reviews and classics like Fahrenheit 451, but I want to read more from Toni Morrison.

Name one thing you are looking forward to experiencing at Stanford.

I look forward to being a maker at Stanford, whether it's making improvements to student life as a leader in ASSU, making an article that's published in Aisthesis, the undergraduate Classics journal, or even making my teammates laugh. I want to graduate having made Stanford's community more vibrant.

Imagine you had an extra hour in the day—how would you spend that time?

"Everyone has 24 hours in a day, even Bill Gates." – Mom. Frankly, it'd be wasteful to keep an extra hour of traveling, creating, and learning to myself. After discovering my advantage over Bill Gates, I'd use it to figure out how I can help others also get an extra hour.

Reader 1

fee waiver, income eligible, parents divorced 2010, no mention of 2nd parent, QBF

HSR: moderate MD, SUGPA 3.85, 1 600-level sequence of Latin for the Classical Diploma, 1 500-level English sequence of English lit electives and a trimester of 500-level Calc

EC: 25 h/w as primary caretake for autistic sister, spent summer at UC-Irvine on classical translations, involved with National Classics Conference, formerly competed with USA Water Polo team at Jr Olympics for 3 years and ranked 15th internationally among middle school golfers at US Kids Jr Golf World Championships, at Exeter, golf team, stugov, classics publication, Certamen team

PE: about family's hardships and how prayer allows her to make sense of it, family goes to Irvine every summer to help her grandparents, well-written, not overdone. Describes herself as the "female reincarnation of Julius Caesar"

[NAME]'s POE is how she excelled in the Classics, pursuing Latin and Greek with depth, all while taking care of significant family responsibilities. [redacted] her academic profile is overall strong in her personal context. Her writing shows IV for Classics, strong writing and engagement with the supplement. Good potential to emerge here.

Reader 2

Confirming R1's ratings, summary assessment, and overall eval. A very strong angular file, augmented by non-cogs and personal strength.

REC: Committee Review

Tags

DIV, QBF

Reader 1 Scores	
Metric	**Score**
Test Rtg	1
HSR	3
Support	3
EC	1
SP-IV	2
Eval	2

Reader 2 Scores	
Metric	**Score**
Test Rtg	1
HSR	3
Support	3
EC	1
SP-IV	2
Eval	2

Profile IV

Iowa

Personal Essay

Few tasks are as intimidating as parallel parking, but for me, this challenge seemed more like a relevant metaphor. For as long as I can remember, my mother would commit to a parking spot and remain steadfast—no matter the constraints. "I swear I can make it," she insisted. However, my mother neglected to consider the vast array of other options, and fell into a convergent mindset.

One time, in particular, is ingrained into my memory. Weekly, my mother and I went to the Farmers' Market. Eyeing a "rock-star parking spot," she haphazardly turned on her blinkers and initiated the park.

"WHAT ARE YOU DOING?" I screamed as cars whizzed past us on the bustling avenue downtown, shaking the Toyota Highlander with the gusts of wind.

"How could we pass up this spot?" she followed up, as if she were naive enough to ignore the surrounding hoards of traffic.

"There are plenty of other spots!" I remarked.

"This spot has our names on it!" she exclaimed.

Therein lies the metaphor: parallel parking means fitting into an enclosed space, just as one tries to fit into and identify with a place in society. The hallmark The Breakfast Club quote struck me as eerily relevant: "You see us as you want to see us—in the simplest of terms, in the most convenient definitions." Even from a young age, I struggled to identify with superlatives that my peers fell into so easily. They were quick to deem themselves as "athletes," "artists," or "academics." In truth, I was all of those things, yet I never conformed; I couldn't seem to locate my single "parking place" in life.

My town championed a conservative approach to personal expression. Classmates ostracized me for only socializing with my female counterparts; fellow swimmers hid my keys after officially coming out in junior year. I soon realized that I would have to deal with small-town closed-mindedness due to my identity.

However, things began falling into place after I immersed myself in the RYLA, when I was chosen to be a team counselor to guide other high school leaders in reaching an enlightened understanding of themselves. The most quintessential component of the conference involves counselor testimonials, where counselors pour out their life stories to expose their vulnerabilities, along with the lessons learned along their journeys. On July 17, I found myself staring into a crowd of three hundred strangers. I felt the same rush of adrenaline and fear fill my head as I flashed back to the frightening experience of my mother's arbitrary parking scene.

I finally built up the courage to unapologetically say, "I'm gay," in front of people I'd never met before. I was showered with hugs and support from people I'd never met before— something I'd never experienced before. I had been so used to the judgment and shunning after I told people my secret, that

I'd been completely desensitized to acceptance. It struck me — there's a bigger world outside of small-town Iowa.

Though growing up in rural Iowa posed significant struggles, it made me the person I am today — full of grit and perseverance. Since rejecting conformity, I unapologetically live in my own terms. I am proud of my diverse background and interests; they make me who I am and reaffirm the values I uphold.

Realizing that upholding identities that deviated from society's norm was not something to fear, I choose to share my story, rather than fear it. Similar to my brief run-in with death, I still feel equivalent emotions whenever I become vulnerable about my background. However, the impact I can have on others is immeasurable."

Intellectual Vitality

"From a young age, I loved letters. The endless combinations of phonemes have always captivated me. Bananagrams transformed from a leisurely activity into a high-stakes competition between whomever my opponent was — much like moving from intramurals to the Olympics. I am additionally infatuated with cultural appreciation. Going to cultural festivals across the United States still retains its status as one of my favorite mainstays. The perfect combination between both interests is the increasingly prevalent study of sociolinguistics. Recently, it has particularly caught my eye because it uniquely combines the variations in language and reveals phrases that are acquired from other cultures and dialects.

Pop culture colloquialisms often reflect appropriation from minority cultures, which is compellingly relevant, yet nothing is done to correct these faults. The spread of social media has appropriated black culture and is often taken out of context. In looking further into this aspect of language, phrases that use incorrect verb tenses solely for the effect fall under this category—like "it be like that" or "the bus been late."

With the enlightenment into sociolinguistics, society can be more cognizant of the language that is used and avoid offensive colloquialisms. Sociolinguistics hold the key to restructure underlying racism in everyday conversations. Through research and surveying my school, I found that the majority of people don't notice the problem; however, insight into where particular phrases may be harmful to marginalized groups is one of the many things necessary to curb systemic racism."

Roommate Essay

"Hey, roomie!

I'm sure most people don't believe in fate, but I do. I hope this doesn't come across as creepy, but we were a match made in … well not necessarily Heaven, but the comparable roommate-matching committee. With the complex algorithms, I'm sure we've been both assigned and hand-picked to live together, to teach each other something valuable.

Due to my inquisitive nature, I am, of course, pondering what you have been assigned to teach me. Maybe, you'll teach me to adopt a sensible sleep schedule, and to abandon my insomniac tendencies. Maybe, you'll teach me that not all straight men are homophobic (I'm joking, mostly). Maybe, you'll compliment my unbridled passion of politics by challenging my views—teaching me to articulate my thoughts more coherently. For you, I'll pass along my Midwestern kindness! Naturally, I've been told I have a compassionate persona—you can be the judge of that.

I hope we become the Amy Poehler and Tina Fey of Stanford, perhaps, in male form. Our humor and dynamic duo-ness will be simultaneously envied and craved by our classmates.

Dibs on the window-bunk! "

What is Meaningful to You?

""He asks too many questions," my eighth-grade Natural Sciences teacher sighed at Parent-Teacher conferences.

While my peers have readily conformed, or accepted certain statements, I'm the consistent "why" in and out of the classroom. I reject the response: "because it's always been this way."

I took this persona upon me, especially when asking myself why civics—another meaningful component of my life—is not stressed in high school. After consulting with local professors, compiling studies from surrounding schools, and comparing policies from various states' codes to create a curriculum, I advocated for the imperative class of "Contemporary Issues" to the ICSD School Board. "We've never done anything like this before," they said, as they refused my proposal.

After the ominous rejection, I regrouped. "If my school doesn't have the fiscal appropriations, how can this be accomplished?"

I asked myself. So, I am currently advocating for such reforms on the state-level. With the legislative session approaching, I ask lawmakers to make a specified-fund, allocating funds to schools willing to be "democracy schools," similar to those in Illinois.

I came back to my school still noticing the discrepancy of activities for civic-minded students, like me. Interested in diplomacy and discourse, I founded my school's Model UN curriculum to make this avenue a reality.

The unsatisfactory response of "this is how we've always done it" simply does not cut it. I believe that innovation is always prevalent; we, as a society, can find better ways of executing tasks by questioning the status quo."

What is the most significant challenge that society faces today?

"Vendettas

1. divide groups through

2. unnecessary, petty conflict, with the sole purpose of

3. vengeance and deceit,

4. creating gridlock (most notably with politics), causing

5. neglectful sentiments, lacking empathy and consideration of the common good,

6. creating a negative aura to run rampant throughout society."

How did you spend your last two summers?

Both summers, I facilitated a transformative summer-camp experience, dubbed RYLA: a week-long immersion into leadership exercises, personality examinations, and counselor testimonials. I realized my impactful and inspiring story needed to be shared—I came out as gay, and revealed my family's financial struggles—and it influenced others to embrace their adversities.

What historical moment or event do you wish you could have witnessed?

Concurrent with my fascination of European History and the advancement of human rights, I would like to retroactively witness the Helsinki Accords. Here, the first efforts to establish universal, fundamental freedoms originated, paving the groundwork for future human rights agencies. I'd sit, of course, next to Helmut Schmidt, renowned diplomat.

What five words best describe you?

Sincere, Tenaciously Ambitious, Noteworthy Fortitude, Objectively Resilient, Developing ...

When the choice is yours, what do you read, listen to, or watch?

"I'm a journalism junkie.

I both enter and exit sleep gripping my phone with CNN illuminating its screen.

The opening sequence to The Daily subconsciously stimulates my thoughts through Classical Conditioning.

I cannot help but to break out in dance to the NPR piano interludes."

Name one thing you are looking forward to experiencing at Stanford.

SIEPR piques my interests of an interdisciplinary, yet cohesive path in economic policies. The underlying principles coincide with my self-goals, culminating in diversity of perspectives and specialties, coming together to improve lives through policy. With SIEPR, I hope to become a research assistant and gain knowledge of international trade policies.

Imagine you had an extra hour in the day—how would you spend that time?

I would spend an extra hour honing in my religious beliefs. I self-identify as agnostic, but attended Methodist church in youth, sang Lutheran hymns in adolescence, and annually embark on summer mission trips with Presbyterians. An extra hour would allow me to articulate my beliefs, and find the fitting denomination.

Reader 1

"PE: owning identity, politically active in a conservative community, metaphor of parallel parking, quirky but it works

IVE: interested in fields like sociolinguistics as a tool to curb systemic racism

SM: challenging status quo and acting until you get change

Uses voice to inspire others to find their own

EC: Public policy admirable work

HSR: DE yr 12

[NAME] is one to take"

Reader 2

"passion for policy shines through entire application, social science IV & passionate and caring SP.

EC: IA House of Reps Page—slight decrease in rigor

distance traveled, passion, IV, SP, strong academics, and impact on community leads me to admit

In a better resourced area, he'd be a 2"

Interviewer Comments

IV—2; Depth + Commitment—1; Character + Self Presentation—3

Tags

IV (x2), SP (x2)

Reader 1 Scores	
Metric	**Score**
Test Rtg	1
HSR	3
Support	2
EC	2
SP-IV	2
Eval	2

Reader 2 Scores	
Metric	**Score**
Test Rtg	1
HSR	3
Support	2
EC	2
SP-IV	2
Eval	2-

Profile V

Hawaii

Personal Essay

You might think it's childish, but I enjoy watching Japanese anime and Chinese, Korean, Japanese, and Spanish soap operas in my free time. Sure, much of the anime I watch is directed toward children, but the stories are lighthearted, and the dialogue is easy to understand. I have learned most of my Japanese from these shows that cause me to laugh, cry, and smile uncontrollably. Of course, not everything I watch is targeted at children: although I don't understand as much of the dialogue, the stories of anime for teenagers and adults usually appeal to me more. However, when I'm watching anime with more difficult vocabulary, I find that I'm not actually learning much Japanese. Even when I watch Spanish shows, whose dialogue I completely understand, I still pick up a few new terms here and there because I just listen to the dialogue, but in anime I find myself only reading English subtitles and neglecting the Japanese words I hear. In other words, I tend to subconsciously sacrifice language-learning in favor of plot comprehension when presented with subtitles in a language I understand well. At this rate, I'd never be able to fully understand a Japanese film, and all the untranslated meanings and nuances would continue to be lost on me.

Once I discovered my unfavorable tendency, I decided to watch anime unsubtitled; if I wanted to understand everything, I'd rewatch it with subtitles afterward. On the first viewing, it's frustrating not understanding what's going on most of the time, but all of my attention is devoted to listening to the dialogue and understanding as much as possible. As I listen, I pick up new words, grammar structures, and the quirks of different dialects. After making this change, I began wondering whether I should have done so sooner, and a question popped up: When would be the best time for someone to stop using subtitles when watching foreign language videos in order to maximize the learning potential? I began to wonder whether such a cutoff point existed, and so I came up with a research proposal.

I propose conducting an experiment with participants who are learning a foreign language and who represent different levels of knowledge in that language, ranging from beginner to advanced. The experimenter would record the participants' ages, the range of each participant's vocabulary, the types of grammar structures he or she recognizes, and how much of the final comprehension test he or she is able to complete correctly. The experimenter would then divide the participants into two groups that are balanced in terms of the number of people representing each level. Both groups would be shown a number of films in the target language over the span of a number of days. One group would watch the films with English subtitles, while the other would watch the same films unsubtitled. At the end of each film, the participants would answer questions on both listening and plot comprehension, and without any special instruction or studying, they would complete their role by retaking the final test. I believe this would help determine how much of a language a person should know before being able to decisively switch to unsubtitled videos and minimize the amount of time wasted learning less than he or she should be.

My Japanese teachers have told me that I have a native Japanese speaker's accent, and it's all because of my anime-watching hobby. If I could get even more out of the shows I love, why wouldn't I try? I'm sure there are others who feel similarly, though I understand that most people would never sacrifice subtitles because interest in the plot keeps them watching a show. However, I believe that films can become infinitely more interesting when words' meanings aren't inevitably lost in translation. Viewers, as well as the linguistic community, would benefit from a better understanding of language learning using films.

Intellectual Vitality

The interconnection between different languages fascinates me. People can link multiple languages together without even knowing it; while growing up, if I didn't know a Spanish word, I could often use English to derive it. No one had told me that English and Spanish were closely related, yet I sensed it naturally. Recently, I listened in on a French teacher's conversation with her student in French and stood off to the side nonchalantly, hoping to pick up a few words and figure out the gist of their conversation based on the Spanish I know, and for the most part it worked. I just can't help myself when it comes to language; I suppose I'm like a girl in love longing to learn about her crush. One tidbit and I feel immense satisfaction and giddiness, often having to hide my grin in public.

Additionally, using language to communicate with computers (e.g., speech-to-text functions, virtual assistants, etc.) has become central to our use of cell phones, laptops, and other technology with which we interact on a daily basis. Whenever I think, "This feature could be improved," or "It would be nice if this feature were included," I feel frustrated that I don't know how to make those changes. This is why I want to study computational linguistics and launch myself into the vast field of AI. I can't wait to see what kind of technology will be created in the future, and I also want to make discoveries of my own.

Roommate Essay

Hello, new roommate! I hope we'll get along well together! Here are just a few things about me: first of all, my desk may seem disorganized, but I'll know exactly where everything is. A teacher has once even called my notes "organized chaos." When I'm in the room, I'll usually be quietly listening to music through my earbuds while doing work or browsing the web. I hope you won't mind if I hum and sing sometimes. I also like to watch comedic Asian dramas and anime, so please don't mind me if I'm grinning weirdly. I might also burst out in laughter all of a sudden if I'm unable to hold it in. Maybe we'll have similar interests? I would love to watch some shows together with you and hear your opinion! By the way, are you fluent in another language? If so, by all means please teach me sometime! I would also love to hear about the customs of the place from which you come. In return, I'll tell you about Chinese and Spanish culture since my family is a mix of the two. I look forward to meeting you soon!

What is Meaningful to You?

I've had Piggy since I was a baby. She's a little, pink stuffed baby cow with a decorative diaper, a snout that flaps, and curly ribbons on her head. Please don't think too deeply about her name; I really thought she was a pig. I couldn't sleep without her as a child, and she's accompanied me on all my family trips. We've trekked through jungles and crossed rivers in Ecuador, ridden in my grandmother's bicycle basket and strolled through the night market in Taiwan, and gotten lost on the streets of Japan together. Piggy's battle scars have long been sewn up by my mom, but they are still visible reminders of our journeys together. Piggy was my companion, and I've grown attached to her. She still sits on a shelf in my room, waiting for more love and adventure. Sometimes, I pick her up just to look at her, play with her curled ribbons the way I used to as a child, and recall the memories she represents. Now that I'm going off to new places to experience new things, I'll take Piggy along with me so that she doesn't miss a thing.

What is the most significant challenge that society faces today?

Not Provided.

How did you spend your last two summers?

Not Provided.

What historical moment or event do you wish you could have witnessed?

Not Provided.

What five words best describe you?

Not Provided.

When the choice is yours, what do you read, listen to, or watch?

Not Provided.

Name one thing you are looking forward to experiencing at Stanford.

Not Provided.

Imagine you had an extra hour in the day—how would you spend that time?

Not Provided.

Reader 1

Academic: ... but I see 6 or 6.5 solids each year and 2x for lang. in 9-11, 3x for lang. in 12th. Has taken heavy load of humanities APs (2x eng, ush, phys, calc, an, cs). APs missing are chem, bio, etc. Currently Japanese 4H, Chinese 4H, and Spanish 3H (spoken at home).

EC: creating an app for her HS for lang dept. Helps students choose their for lang. track. Global Issues Netwk, 9-12. FPT, Vol for Japanese and Chinese transl of web novels. Student notes that long commute to school (2 hr each way) accounts for her lack of ability to join clubs)

Essays:

PE: proposes experiment to study how best to learn for lang. through film.

IV: Innate interest in lang and learning them through non-formal channels; interest in computational linguistics/AI.

MW: stuffed cow triggers memories of journeys together

Reader 2

Leaning away. ECs very limited. Academically competitive, but SPIV could be higher. Ideas not really groundbreaking. Interest in FL very evident. Don't feel that she will emerge, but defer to TM to consider with school group and context

Tags

DIV, GEN1

Reader 1 Scores	
Metric	**Score**
Test Rtg	2
HSR	3
Support	3
EC	4
SP-IV	3
Eval	2-

Reader 2 Scores	
Metric	**Score**
Test Rtg	2
HSR	4
Support	3
EC	3
SP-IV	3
Eval	3+

Profile VI

Oregon

Personal Essay

The hardest thing I've ever done was tell the truth. Sitting across from my father in an eight by ten room, I had to look him in the eyes and tell him I didn't want to have a relationship with him. Over and over and over.

Statistically, this makes me an anomaly. The instances of children rejecting parents are so rare that hardly anyone knew what to do when, during my parents' divorce proceedings, I announced I didn't want a relationship with my father. Most involved believed I was too young to understand the implications of what I was asking for, but to me it was the most sensical thing I could do. For as long as I can remember, my father has been a toxic presence in my life. Someone who belittled me when I needed understanding, dismissed me when I needed help, and chose anger and unpredictability when I needed stability and safety. I'd already been exposed to so much anger, abuse, and toxicity, that even at 11 years old, I saw he was not being a dad. I knew if I were to grow into a happy and healthy adult, he couldn't be part of my journey.

For the next four years I faced what felt like a Sisyphean task. Surrounded by people who had more power than I did and couldn't fathom where I was coming from, I was accused multiple times of exaggerating or even simply lying about my experiences. During this time, I carried the weight of a battle waged between a subconscious that desperately wanted a dad and a conscious that knew he couldn't be one. There were numerous times when I considered giving in, thinking it would be the easiest option. The experience was enough to make me feel like I was going crazy, but I knew I had to keep going. Before each counseling session, I paused outside the door, collecting the strength I needed and telling myself I could soldier on.

It was only when we were sent to a court-appointed therapist that I was given a platform to unabashedly share what I felt. At the end of these sessions, she wrote a report that said I was not only able to see the ways in which the relationship was unhealthy but was also able to clearly articulate them. Thanks to her, I was granted my wish. After it all, I got to live in a happy and loving home with my mom, where I continue to feel understood, supported, stable, and safe.

To get to this point was the hardest thing I've ever done, but I wouldn't take a minute of it back. It was the most formative experience of my childhood, making me into the resilient and principled young woman I am today. At my age, I already know just how much power my voice can have to advocate for myself and how much strength I have. I know that no matter how difficult something is, and how unlikely an ending seems, there are better days waiting on the other side. I know too that no one, not even my father, is entitled to my respect or worth giving up my values. The most important lesson I've learned though is I don't need to let pain define me. Hardship is a fact of life, and the way I see it, there are two options: letting it defeat me or letting it teach me. I'd be lying if I said I carry none of it with me today, but I go on. There are still tinges of sadness at the loss of a father, but in those moments I remind myself of the lessons it gave me and the strength it has brought out. When something gets hard, I think back to that little girl, standing outside the door, and I soldier on.

Intellectual Vitality

For the first ten years of my life, I was fortunate enough to attend a French immersion school. There, I was surrounded by teachers who barely spoke English and came from places like France, Senegal, Canada, and Morocco. My classmates were from equally far-flung corners of the globe. In that microcosm of the world I was given the chance to hear their worldviews. The great diversity in thoughts and backgrounds created an environment where I was constantly met with cultures and stories far removed from my own. I was fascinated by everything the people I was surrounded by had to offer.

With this, I grew an insatiable hunger. When I understood that such a well-developed, enriching, community came from sharing the French language, I saw that other languages could unlock more doors. French turned into Spanish into Swedish into Arabic. Each is like a passport, making countries filled with culture and stories accessible to me. New windows into the world also come with a healthy dose of humility. Realizing the world that immediately surrounds me isn't the world, I don't feel insignificant, rather I get excited. It means there's always potential to talk to one more person, hear one more song, see one more painting, taste one more dish. All I need to do is learn the language that unlocks it.

Roommate Essay

Dear future roommate,

Before you learn anything else about me, it's important you know I'm an only child. Despite my never ending war waged against stereotypes, some of the side effects of only childhood are unavoidable. To start, I've never had to share a sleeping space like this before, so while you try to cram for that Spanish final late at night you may hear me singing in French in my sleep. I also have far too many books to be contained by shelving and we could need to use some as furniture. Don't worry about a mess though, being a bit of a control freak I will obsessively sort everything from snacks to stationery into labelled bins.

Don't run in the other direction though, because being a roommate to an only child has its perks. Having you by my side, I'm excited to have someone to share in my spur of the moment puns, French skincare, and movie collection. I'm the perfect teammate during game night because playing against my mom my whole life, I've learned how to beat adults(!) at Scrabble. I'll also always understand if you need space and want the room to yourself, because I'll know how great that can be. Most importantly, I am the most loyal friend you could have. My friends make up for siblings I never had, so I see you as family. You and I, we're in this adventure together. I'm excited to get started.

What is Meaningful to You?

This past fall when I underwent jaw surgery, among the many pieces of advice I received on my recovery, I was told that laughing could hurt. A lot. I learned that this was indeed true as I spent the next week being taken care of by my mom and grandma, laughing constantly. The three of us are inseparable and time spent with the two of them makes up some of my most cherished memories, giving me more adventures in just 17 years than I could ask for in a lifetime. Whether it's something as banal as learning you can make whipped cream in a blender or as wild as spending six days at the Louvre, they've enriched my life with so much joy and love.

Having three generations of strong women supporting one another is a gift I feel fortunate to have, as are the lessons I learn from them. My grandma, an 84 year old ex-teacher, is a veritable encyclopedia, yet she is always curious about the world around her. In her, I see that no matter who you are there's something new to learn. My mom has sacrificed so much for me and my future, and continues to do so without expecting anything in return. In her, I've learned that unconditional love is real and infinitely powerful. These women give me hope, showing me that not only is there good in the world but that I too have the power to spread it to others.

What is the most significant challenge that society faces today?

In the face of seemingly ubiquitous injustice many become frozen, not knowing where to begin. Others may rely on hope, waiting for someone else to take action. It's important to not do what is comfortable and instead do what is right: fighting for what we believe in.

How did you spend your last two summers?

I attended nationals for dance in New York and Las Vegas, travelled the Rhone with my Grandma, interned with the Governor, saw Harry Styles in concert, reorganized my house, attended a Mercy Corps program, read and watched everything I couldn't during school, and had a few sunburns.

What historical moment or event do you wish you could have witnessed?

I wish I could have been at the drafting of the UN Declaration of Human Rights. I am inspired thinking of all those countries coming together, despite political and cultural differences. They had a common goal to serve humanity, make the world better, and take action to do just that.

What five words best describe you?

Tenacious, creative, lively, caring, positive

When the choice is yours, what do you read, listen to, or watch?

Read: Refinery29, Le Monde, the New York Times, The Sympathizer, The Family Fang, Midnight in the Garden of Good and Evil, Gone Girl

Listen: French rap, Kendrick Lamar, the Mamma Mia soundtrack, Lorde, Alt-J, classic rock.

Watch: Arrested Development, the West Wing, John Mulaney, 90s thrillers, Wes Anderson movies

Name one thing you are looking forward to experiencing at Stanford.

Nerd Nation, where dining hall chats on whether math proves the existence of God and games of catch in the quad analyzing Noam Chomsky are normal, sounds like paradise. Being amidst thousands who are constantly questioning and just as engaged as I am is where I want to be.

Imagine you had an extra hour in the day—how would you spend that time?

I would take an extra hip hop class. The energy in a well taught class is so great that I can practically feel the air buzzing. There's also something cathartic about jumping around, embodying a cooler version of myself with all my next steps planned out.

Reader 1

Strong application, excellent grades with a full slate. Really admire what she's been through. Impressive pqs. Commitment to helping others. Great fit and addition to SU. She's potentially compelling and I'm leaning in.

Reader 2

She's a budding social scientist as shown through her ECs. SPIV is warm. RME & SME are standard and didn't stand out. She has the chops for SU. Farf is a nice touch but it's just there, she doesn't talk about it. Social Science IV makes itself known in the ECs. Voice in CAPE is strong. Pieces are here but not coming together in a compelling manner, perhaps it's that the file lacks energy.

Tags

DIV, FA

Reader 1 Scores	
Metric	**Score**
Test Rtg	2
HSR	3
Support	3
EC	3
SP-IV	3
Eval	2-

Reader 2 Scores	
Metric	**Score**
Test Rtg	2
HSR	3
Support	3
EC	2
SP-IV	3
Eval	2-

The Academic Powerhouse

Profile I

Indiana

Personal Essay

"Forget placing – I'll be happy if I win anything," she muttered.

"I don't think I have a very good chance," he murmured.

"No way I'll win. Everyone else is too good," yet another mumbled.

With this past year being my first attending the Intel International Science and Engineering Fair, I had hoped my fellow competitors might impart some insights into the judging process and their expectations. However, many of my peers truly believed their only recognition at ISEF would be participation. Although I did not know why at the time, I felt disappointed in them. Why would they consciously disparage their own abilities? We 1800 competitors were supposedly the best from 78 countries.

As judging progressed, the atmosphere in the convention center worsened – smiles became strained, polished speeches lost their sheen, worries prevailed. On the contrary, I was unflustered, energetic, and frankly, enjoying myself. During the small talk that filled the dry spells between interviews, the girl next to me asked, "how can you be so ... self-assured?" Before I could respond, she became preoccupied with a judge, leaving me alone to sort out my thoughts. At the time, I had attributed my composure to years of science fair competitions; yet, many of my peers had been competing for as long as or longer than me.

A few weeks after my third-place finish, many kind congratulations, and an exhausting trip home, I sat outside, enjoying the midday tranquility and reading abstracts of the top projects. Although I couldn't change the outcome of ISEF, I pored over each abstract and analyzed the presenters' posters, extracting the common elements of intelligibility, novelty, and societal significance. I carefully documented each project's advantages over mine, numerous as they were. Although it would take me a few weeks to recognize, that afternoon epitomized the reason for my composure and a defining personality trait – my unnatural response to failure.

Like most competitive people, I strive to win and do not enjoy failure. Whether it was a second-place finish, not supporting my team well, or just making numerous careless mistakes, failures had disheartened me until my tenth-grade state science fair. That year, I had devoted more time and effort than I ever had before with the hopes of winning my first ticket to Intel; consequently, I was crushed when my project was passed over. But—it was that failure which taught me the futility of sulking; misery certainly wasn't going to contribute to my future successes. In light of this experience, I realized I couldn't allow myself to be limited by self-pity.

When most people encounter a superior talent, their typical response is a default to the blame game in order to avoid acknowledging their own weaknesses. My strength lies in consciously removing myself from defeatist emotions when I encounter superiority which could lead to my "failure" – the strength to dispassionately confront and try whatever is necessary to overcome the perceived disparity in potential for success between my betters and me. Ironically, the only reason I can exercise this strength is not because I accept failure, but rather because I want to succeed more than anyone else. My Intel experience revealed the origin of my success – my achievements are not only a product of my failures but also the fact that I am secretly the biggest sore loser I know.

Those who become consumed with resentful jealousy for the victor are not sore losers. I would know as I used to be the embodiment of a vindictive loser and an immodest winner. But, all these competitions, my peers, and my own tenacity have shaped me into a true sore loser – not one with self-deluding optimism or unfounded aspirations, but an individual who refuses to accept personal failures, who eagerly anticipates adversity, and who recognizes that others' triumphs are stepping stones to my own future accomplishments.

Intellectual Vitality

Frankly, most high school courses are not difficult for me. While many courses present novel materials, my conventional methods of studying have been sufficient – reading, memorizing, and applying. I expected my physics class to be no different.

On my first day in Physics I, my teacher, Mr. Beeler, said "memorizing gets you nowhere in this class. If you think you're going to do well by regurgitating formulas, drop this class." I thought I had no reason to believe him – memorizing had enabled me to ace tests and dominate finals; however, my first few physics quizzes proved me wrong. Mr. Beeler was right. Physics demanded a level of true understanding that none of my other classes did.

But more than challenging me to think, Mr. Beeler made physics exciting, dynamic, and even enjoyable. I relished in the class's practical applications – using a slingshot to nail Mr. Beeler with a water balloon, building my own heat engine, getting dizzyingly sick when using a spinning chair to demonstrate conservation of angular momentum. In the following year's course, Physics II, I re-found my childlike sense of wonder through powering a lightbulb using magnetic flux, tinkering around with AC rectifiers, and firing a Gauss rifle.

Each day I understood the universe a little more, but that understanding only drove me to more inquiries. But for once, I was happy to admit I knew little. Physics awakened a dormant, insatiable curiosity I had, and today, I am glad this quest for knowledge has no foreseeable end.

Roommate Essay

Do you like to eat? Great!

Do you like to eat good food? Well, you might be a little out of luck.

My enjoyment in cooking originally came from neither its practicality nor an inherent talent. I picked up cooking thanks to a lecture.

As a typical lazy 4th grader, my parents were often tsk-tsking at my lack of housework. In one of her well-intentioned lectures, my mom went on about how "when I was your age, I already cooked dinner for my parents." Fine, I had thought, how hard can it be? Thanks to years of eating my mom's delicious meals, I generally knew what I liked to eat. My family always kept a variety of foods in the pantry and refrigerator. All left was the cooking bit – which turned into burnt eggs, salt-caked vegetable stir-fries, and resigning to having instant noodles.

Yet, every time my parents weren't home or I woke up early on a weekend, I found myself drawn to the kitchen again. Slowly but surely, I improved. No longer was I making flavorless pasta or rubbery scrambles. While I'm still nowhere as talented as my mom, now I can at least manage not to give myself hypernatremia.

Ironically, I like to cook because I'm terrible at it! But the hobbies I'm worst at are the ones I enjoy the most because I love to work it out. So, if you're an adventurous spirit, and you'll put up with my cooking, cheers! I'm the roommate for you!

What is Meaningful to You?

"Your rook is mine!" I exclaimed with glee, moving my own queen to capture my father's apparently exposed piece.

"Really?" my dad replied as he deftly moved a bishop back to capture my queen.

Groaning at the short-lived nature of my victory, my dad smiled. "You'd do well to remember that not much is truly yours." As a seven-year-old whose primary strategy was to trade evenly, I marveled at the relative depth of my father's strategy. Remembering his words, I managed to beat him a few weeks later. I haven't won since, but I still haven't forgotten his words.

"Not much is truly yours."

When my parents threatened to take away my favorite toys if I didn't eat my vegetables, I learned that my possessions were not always mine.

When I crashed my bike and flew off the handlebars, sustaining a nauseating blow to my head, I learned my body was not always mine.

When I flipped through my digital camera's old photos and see my little brother as a baby, now seven, I learned that time was not always mine.

But, when I confessed to stealing a pack of gum from the store, when I tried remaining calm instead of shouting at my parents, when I tried to listen–not just hear–a friend's problem, I learned my mind is mine. Integrity. Rationality. Empathy. Ultimately, that afternoon chess game is meaningful because it taught me that my principles are the only things I can truly call my own.

What is the most significant challenge that society faces today?

Close-mindedness. As a child, I was taught to move from intolerance to indifference, from indifference to tolerance. Only recently have I recognized the importance of the stage past tolerance, open-mindedness. Though reconciling differences may not be easy, open-mindedness entails a willingness to change and compromise that the modern world demands.

How did you spend your last two summers?

Summer is about learning and self-improvement. Collegiate and creative writing courses and tutoring at my local Kumon center improve my communication. Working/visiting with research labs at Indiana State, University of Georgia, and Toronto satiates my intellectual curiosity. Community volunteering and Friday football games with friends provide a welcome respite.

What historical moment or event do you wish you could have witnessed?

As a true lover of technology and ancient history since my childhood, I wish I could have experienced the construction of Stonehenge. Although the medieval wonder may serve little practical purpose today, understanding the ancient technological and astronomical advancements enabling the mysterious structure's construction would be an unparalleled intellectual treat.

What five words best describe you?

Zealous, Tenacious, Versatile, Rationale, Committed

When the choice is yours, what do you read, listen to, or watch?

I enjoy titles like 1984, The Good Earth, and anything by Michael Crichton. For listening, I love The Great War, Tides of History, The 1975, and BORNS. When I have the remote, I watch Jeopardy!, The Office, House M.D., and MasterChef. But generally, I enjoy whatever my little brother wants!

Name one thing you are looking forward to experiencing at Stanford.

Socially, I'm eagerly anticipating cornerstone campus traditions like the UC Berkeley-Stanford rivalry, getting trapped in the circle of death, and fountain hopping. Academically, I'm looking forward to engaging in high-level research with acclaimed professors and advancing my humanities education so I can develop an interdisciplinary view on the world's issues.

Imagine you had an extra hour in the day—how would you spend that time?

As a second-generation Asian American, I've always considered the disconnect from my relatives when I visit China a personal fault. Although my Mandarin is not completely terrible, I often become lost in even casual conversations. So, with an extra hour, I'd perfect my abilities to speak, read, and write Mandarin.

Reader 1

Reader 1 Review:

Rec: Admit – [NAME]'s POE is Intel award 3rd grad' 17 earth & eng Sci (and many other notable awards).

10/0: 3 ap + 1H + 1

11/0: 4 ap + calc BC

3 ap + 3

10/13 ap 1/7. shares 1/362 w/3 (not sure what the first 10/13 bit is about; 1/362 is my class rank, note that they note that I share this position with 3 other individuals)

Rural community, western IN (home/location)

F college Prof, M Accountant, older sib Northwestern, 7 yr old bro (family)

Intel on drought Sequoias, interest in Geo & Environ, 2 summers college programs, Model UN & Diplomatic Relations & Creative Writing Duke Cryptography & IU Aviation Fundamentals & Eng 107, notes school leader, plays in the symphonic band (solo gold). Strong PQs SPIV shines. (ECs description, no idea what PQs are, maybe personal questions?)

Geo & Env Sci, Public Pol (Potential majors I noted in my application)

Hon: AP scholar, summer progs: Northwestern, Duke, IU, Intel International Sci & Eng 3rd place grand award winner 2017 Earth & Eng. Sciences, 1st IN academy sci talent search, 2017 & 16

SEE List continued in App AIME qualifier, First place AMC 2016

EC: Pres Model UN, Pres Asian Am Club, Cpt Teams, orientation leader and volunteer middle school math tutor, paid math learning center instructor, volunteer Costa Rica trip, pianist, Intern Geospational Research (association NASA develop team to create a fire vulnerability index based on remotely sense "biophysical" data in conj w/sociec data, intern ISU Genomic Advocacy – study novel genes involved in cardiogenesis in fruit flies and their mammalian and vertebrate orthologs. (more shit on ECs; also something fun to note here: when I took this notes I fixed a lot of the spelling errors but I left this paragraph alone. You can see that the reader made a ton of spelling errors which suggests to me they are going through applications quite quickly)

Notes on essays:

PE: failure drives to study and set goals, made me laugh at "secretly the biggest sore loser" sees "others triumphs as stepping stones to my own future accomplishments"

SU: reputed profs SURGE Phil 171 EDUC 193A life skills and interdiscipliary

xhr: learn mandarin

Learn: Physics understanding the universe a little more daily

RM: loves to cook – terrible at it.

Mean: integrity, rationality, empathy

Reader 2

Agree wholeheartedly with R1. Accolades and high awards abound.

[NAME] is a full fledged scientist, yet instead of feeling locked into a life calling, REDACTED is open to considering law which says much about his maturity and overall character.

Writing oozes SPIV and clear POE has [NAME] a standout in this pool of applicants.

Reader 1 Scores	
Metric	**Score**
Test Rtg	1
HSR	3
Support	2
EC	1
SP-IV	1
Eval	1

Reader 2 Scores	
Metric	**Score**
Test Rtg	1
HSR	3
Support	2
EC	1
SP-IV	1
Eval	1

Profile II

Florida

Personal Essay

"???" was the text I got from my mother in response to a photo I sent her on my first day at the Perimeter Institute for Theoretical Physics this summer. The photo was of a chalkboard showing the "proof" $1+2+3 \ldots = -1/12$. What amazed me, and prompted my photo, was that this 'purely' mathematical result is used to show that string theory predicts a universe with 26 spatial dimensions. The idea that we can describe the universe using precise mathematical descriptions has drawn me to theoretical physics. Here is an idea I have questioned: If we were locked in a room, and provided with infinite time to think about pure mathematics, could we discover the laws of the universe? I strongly suspected that the answer is yes.

My suspicion was affirmed when I heard a notable pure mathematician discuss how his research was being used, without his involvement, in fundamental physics years after his papers were published. My view was further strengthened by a lecture I watched in which physicist Richard Feynman humorously noted that physicists often take results from mathematicians, plug in for the case that the number of dimensions is equal to three, and discover new "physical" principles. Given my love for the beauty of simple mathematical descriptions of the universe, and the impracticality of building an Earth-sized particle accelerator to conduct certain physics experiments, the words of these leaders resonated with me. Additionally, theory is exacting and fundamental, but experiments suffer from experimental error and only provide probabilistic results. Thus, if mathematics is the language of physics, physics is a special case of mathematics, and experimentation is expensive and unreliable, perhaps mathematics alone should be used to advance physics.

While relying solely on mathematics would be parsimonious, I began questioning my reasoning during my electrodynamics course at the University of Miami. On the first day, we used equations from multivariable calculus to write alternate forms of Maxwell's equations of electricity and magnetism. I learned that while we used mathematics to transform the equations, the equations themselves are dictated by experimental results. From this, I came to realize that perhaps mathematics is a tool we use in physics to describe our knowledge, but it does not allow us to verify new knowledge. This summer, at the Perimeter Institute, I talked to my friend Qiushi extensively about my original question. A few days later, the director of the institute showed us a formula describing everything we know about physics. I was astonished that such a formula existed and asked how could we mathematically prove that this equation is correct. He said that while we have a mathematical model of the universe, we could not have come upon this equation if we had 10 million years on an island with no ability to experiment. That is, without experimentation we would have no ability to constrain mathematical possibilities. Qiushi and I smiled at each other in awe.

More recently, my views regarding my question have evolved. I understand that pure mathematics and experimental physics are both essential tools for understanding the true nature of the universe at all of its levels. On the last day of my time at the Perimeter Institute, I sent my mother another picture, this time one of me holding the Nobel prize in physics that had been received by the Sudbury Neutrino Observatory for verifying the existence of the neutrino. I had a smile on my face in the photo after learning that the researchers who received it had found that the neutrino does exist but that, counter to what the current model predicted, it has mass. I now appreciate that while pure mathematics provides a useful model, experimental physics is necessary to reveal which aspects of the model are incorrect or incomplete. My mother's response back to that photo was, "How cool!" I agree.

Intellectual Vitality

In 9th grade I took to an EdX microeconomics course. One lecture focused on how we could use a simple budget constraint and a given utility function to find out what an ideal consumer would purchase. This solution was interesting, but I felt that the model must be limited because the context was so constrained (i.e., prices were constant and only 2 goods were being purchased at a time). I wanted to expand this model to be more generalizable using a concept I learned from multivariable calculus, lagrange multipliers. I saw a potential application wherein, for an arbitrary utility function, we could use lagrange multipliers to create a system of equations that could be solved using a computer. The solution would tell us how much of each item to buy to maximize the utility function (e.g., representing a person's happiness) given the budget constraints for that person. This example highlighted to me how we could use mathematical models (albeit a very simple one, in this case), to solve social and economic problems. This was my first enticing glimpse into the modeling of arbitrary systems and the creativity required to allow such models to generalize. As the course progressed, I continued to find examples and considered how to expand on economic models using mathematics. It is exciting to think that as I gain more knowledge in math and physics, I can be better equipped to model scenarios of greater complexity (e.g., financial systems).

Roommate Essay

Dear Roommate,

Here are six things about me to help you get to know me better.

First, as a competitive Rubik's cube solver, I am often solving some sort of twisty puzzle to take my mind off of other things. I will try to keep the noise level to a minimum, so please pardon the clicks and pops.

Second, I do not speak Russian but I enjoy listening to Russian electronic pop music. If you speak Russian, you may need to inform me of the painfully cheesy lyrics.

Third, I occasionally talk out loud but don't worry it is mainly just me practicing random Chinese words to get the tones right.

Fourth, I like to make meticulous plans for myself at night. You may see me writing notes in my planner at late hours.

Fifth, I take a biotin pill twice daily. 50 years ago, I would have died as an infant because of a genetic condition which is fully remedied by taking biotin. This gives me great respect for the medical profession and medical research.

Sixth, I have a dream catcher hanging above my bed. In the Chippewa Tradition it is supposed to get rid of bad dreams. I like this reminder of my ancestry at the beginning and end of my day.

One last thing to know about me is that even though chance has thrown us together, I will look after you and have your back when times get tough.

Best,

[NAME]

What is Meaningful to You?

Suffering exists, and we have a moral obligation to reduce it by our actions in the World. Being Chippewa, I am proud of my heritage, my indigenous ancestry and the people of my tribe. I am both saddened and emboldened by the struggles and hardships that have been placed upon my ancestors that still affect my tribal community today. My ancestral background drives my interest in effective altruism (EA), doing the most good possible with the resources we have been given. Part of the appeal for EA for me is that 'good' can be characterized quantitatively. This feature allows us to measure, aim for, and achieve the most good in a tangible manner.

I feel strongly that my efforts in life should aim to do the most good in the world. While many following the EA movement preach trying to make the most money to donate to charity, I feel this way of thinking cannot bring about necessary structural change or support innovation. I learned at the Perimeter Institute that 25% of the world's GDP growth during the 20th century has been attributable to advances in theoretical physics. The number of lives saved, technology made possible, and utility gained is truly astounding. Thus, my interest in pursuing physics is motivated not only by my deep interest in the topic, but by a desire to make an impact within my community and in the world. I wish to uplift both.

What is the most significant challenge that society faces today?

Climate change. It is a cliché, but that does not make it less real. Motivated by a moral impetus to make personal choices to promote sustainability, I became vegan in 6th grade. Beyond my lifestyle decisions, my academic and professional goals are to make physics breakthroughs to solve this challenge.

How did you spend your last two summers?

2017: AP Chemistry JHU CTY, Royal Palms Tennis Academy Camp, Quantum Mechanics(EdX) Georgetown, Multivariable Calculus(MIT OpenCourseWare)

2018: Perimeter Institute ISSYP Program(4% Acceptance Rate), Chinese Bridge Summer Program, Writing [NAME]'s Guide to AP Physics C: Mechanics and Electrodynamics Study Guides

What historical moment or event do you wish you could have witnessed?

The first encounter between the Indigenous Americans of North America and the white Europeans. How did they communicate? What were their first responses and facial expressions? Was there more curiosity or aggression? Wonderment or anxiety? A comparable situation is unlikely to happen again.

What five words best describe you?

Driven, persistent, humorous, altruistic, inquisitive

When the choice is yours, what do you read, listen to, or watch?

Read: "Bury My Heart at Wounded Knee", "The Elements of Differential Geometry", "Life, Death, and Neurosurgery", "Justice: What's The Right Thing to Do", "How Not To Die"(nutrition book)

Listen: EDM, This American Life, Planet Money, The Majority Report, Joe Rogan Podcast

Watch: Planet Earth, Mathologer, Rae's Medical School Vlogs

Name one thing you are looking forward to experiencing at Stanford.

I would like to be part of a research team at the Stanford Institute for Theoretical Physics (e.g., lab of Dr. Leonard Susskind, whose work I learned about at ISSYP) investigating quantum gravity or quantum foundations. I want to create new knowledge and disseminate it in a peer-reviewed article.

Imagine you had an extra hour in the day—how would you spend that time?

I would finish reading "Options, Futures, and Other Derivatives" by John C. Hull. I understand that quantitative finance involves many applications of physics and many modern hedge funds are being run by physicists. This leaves me interested in this topic and wanting to learn the basics.

Reader 1

Red admit- at least WL; soft lean in

POE-aca strenght, early grad, IV

Pause: SP, warmth

Overall vstrong app-testing + aca esp given context, aca powerhouse

Writing std overall, light in depth and energy

SPIV-flat, holds back app

EC's varied light in leadership and campus engagement, not particularly compelling

SPIV-strong

app-overall strong

Reader 2

Rec: on the fence, slight lean in

POE-sheer academic strength

IV-strong

Questioning whether team player and if can contribute strongly to the community

SD-pause

Writing-lacks depth or emotion

overall-leaning in but only slightly

Reader 1 Scores	
Metric	**Score**
Test Rtg	1
HSR	2
Support	3+
EC	3+
SP-IV	3+
Eval	2-

Reader 2 Scores	
Metric	**Score**
Test Rtg	1
HSR	2
Support	3+
EC	3+
SP-IV	3+
Eval	2-

Profile III

Virginia

Personal Essay

"I do it myself.

My parents like to joke that "I do it myself" was my first sentence. Even as a two-year-old, I was stubbornly independent. One of my earliest memories was memorizing "The Hungry Caterpillar" in an attempt to teach myself to read. When I was five years old, I tried to ride a bike without training wheels. Several falls, some tears, and a few hours later I had figured out how to wobble through our backyard.

In school, I never asked questions, instead opting to find a book. I was afraid that, had I asked someone, I would have seemed less intelligent. This was a habit which continued well into high school, fueled by my fear of a challenge and the familiarity of my intellectual and social "comfort zones."

After my sophomore year, I began to conduct independent research at a local hospital. I was generally left alone with my work, relying mostly on journal articles and textbooks for answers. My advisor, mentoring six other students, was perfectly happy with this approach, giving me a high degree of freedom once I'd learned the basics.

Still, with this freedom came mistakes. They were small — a dropped bottle of culture medium or accidental contamination of cells — but I grew increasingly frustrated with each complication. Finally, I asked for help, and my experiments began to work. With each successful procedure, I gained more knowledge and became more comfortable. Though I preferred to work alone, when I couldn't figure something out I was less afraid to ask a question. I finished the project and continued onto competitions, where I found my independence to be one of my strengths. By learning the mechanisms behind each experiment and decision in the lab, I was able to confidently communicate my results to judges and the public.

A few months later I started in a new lab and felt like a naive child again. Even making media, which was once the simplest of tasks, took hours because I didn't know where the materials were. Not wanting to bother my coworkers, I would walk through the lab trying to find things myself — not the most efficient of processes. It reached its culmination when I found an error in my explanation of the previous project. The cell line, which I thought I'd extensively vetted, was incompetent for viral replication, a fact on which my entire discussion was hanging. I felt like a fraud and quickly began to spiral.

What if I didn't do anything right? What if all of my results are invalid? Am I truly a fraud?

The thoughts raced through my mind, but I didn't tell anyone. Then, finally, I decided to mention the fears to my mentor. And what she said next changed my view of research, and life, in general:

"[NAME], have you heard of imposter syndrome?" she asked. I shook my head, and she explained, "Imposter syndrome is incredibly common, especially in research. You find a flaw in your data and obsess over it, comparing your work to that of your peers, critiquing your own research and tearing yourself down in the process."

I looked at her blankly. Though I didn't want to admit it, that was exactly how I had felt at the time.

"You made a mistake, but you're also not the first person to do so," she continued. "You can't know everything, and you certainly don't have to be an expert."

Slowly, I began to realize she was right. Maybe I did make a mistake, but it was okay. It's normal to ask for advice, to share doubts, and to make countless mistakes, because that's how we learn. Since then, I've spoken up in my lab, asked for help with protocols, and turned to more than just books and prior knowledge for questions. And, despite my lifelong notion, I can't, and shouldn't have to, "do it myself."

Intellectual Vitality

"Why isn't a virus living?" was the question I asked in my 10th grade biology class. My teacher rattled off a simple reply, but I wasn't satisfied. Returning home, I scoured an old textbook for answers, and ended up with more questions. While reading, I stumbled across a virus called Epstein-Barr virus (EBV). Having not heard of it, I turned to Google. The rest is history.

EBV has, more or less, been a fixture in my life since that fateful day. For most people, EBV infection never poses an issue, with mono being its major presentation. However, the right conditions can catalyze tumor development, cardiomyopathy, and neurodegeneration. The thing I strive to understand is— why?

I can talk incessantly about my work with anyone willing to listen (just ask my family!). The intricacies of the virus are as exciting as the Final Four. If variety is the spice of life, EBV is my saffron.

So, more often than not, I'm reading, thinking, or writing about EBV. My floor is covered with notes scribbled on scraps of paper, and the lab has become my second home. My latest experiment has been meticulously outlined on my bedroom mirror. The hypothesis: reactivation of the virus in tumor cells promotes blood vessel growth, allowing the cancer to spread to other parts of the body.

What started as a simple question two years ago, has today grown into a complex, confusing, and exciting journey through EBV's mysteries, which live in my mind every day.

Roommate Essay

Dear future roommate,

If you read that to the tune of Meghan Trainor's "Dear Future Husband" then you're not alone. Not that I like the song (my taste is more of an eclectic mix between alternative, acoustic, and electronic club remixes), but my sister and I have a tendency of unintentionally putting words to music.

That's just for starters though …

I love food. I'll try pretty much anything, like turtle soup, frog legs, or bone marrow! It's a good bet our room would be stocked with snacks from Trader Joe's (mochi and trail mix are my favorites!)

Coffee gets its own category. My favorite local baristas know my name, favorite drink, and what time I come in at. The research lab where I work has a Keurig dedicated to the delicious "bean juice" too!

Speaking of the lab—I really like science. It's my second home and I probably talk about my research a little too much. So, if (when) that happens, tell me and I promise I'll stop... or make a cringey joke, for which I apologize in advance.

Late night... or midday... de-stress dance parties will be frequent. Also, I'll definitely FaceTime my dog... she's a three-legged, blue-eyed sheepadoodle named Marsonne (after a french wine) whom I adore.

So, to recap: if you sing your sentences, love snacks and coffee, like to talk, and don't mind bad jokes or dogs... we're going to get along great!

See you next fall!

[NAME]

What is Meaningful to You?

In first grade, I wrote my first ever school paper: "How to Make Wine." Unsurprisingly, my parents received a phone call from my perplexed teacher. Unbeknownst to her, "making wine" was part of my life, having grown up helping my parents in our family vineyard.

Each summer, I've spent weeks working diligently in the vineyard with my family, pulling leaves, tucking branches, and trying to keep the vines healthy. Fall arrives, and our friends and family come to help harvest. Like clockwork, the cycle continues each year. The days blur together in an endless stream of routine—pull, prune, pick, repeat. However, we remain focused and persevere, knowing the crop will prosper under our care.

The grapes are an extension of our family—we tend them, and they reward us accordingly. Doing things the proper way (even though it may take longer) gives tangible results, like the sweet juice which trickles from the press after a long day of harvesting.

I've grown up with those vines. My parents' ideology, of putting in the extra time and effort into a task, has been subtly instilled into my being. Whether I'm working on a problem set with friends, or collaborating on a research project, I advocate that we take the extra time to understand the process and work together. Unconsciously, the vineyard, my home, has taken seed in my soul, helping to shape me just as I have helped shape it.

What is the most significant challenge that society faces today?

Immunotherapy, novel drugs, groundbreaking surgeries, and personalized therapies—all are now at the forefront of medicine. And yet, access is limited to those with means. Some of the most devastating diseases—cancer and infections—occur with greater frequency in developing nations. How can we increase access to life-saving treatments around the globe?

How did you spend your last two summers?

The methodical "click" of my pruning snips in the vineyard was intertwined with the snap of a micro-pipette tip disposal at lab. Weekends were filled with coffees, spontaneous dancing, and failed cooking attempts with friends. Relaxing and tanning (or burning) on the beach offered the perfect ending to my summers.

What historical moment or event do you wish you could have witnessed?

A petri dish of mold is sitting on the countertop—another failed experiment. And yet, instead of scrapping it, Alexander Fleming decided to investigate some of its properties, realizing the bacteria on the plate was dying. A simple mistake, but one that revolutionized the face of medicine as we know it.

What five words best describe you?

1. Inquisitive

2. Loquacious

3. Quirky

4. Driven

5. Persistent

When the choice is yours, what do you read, listen to, or watch?

Read: The Da Vinci Code, Frankenstein's Cat, Outliers, Tuesdays with Morrie, John Grisham, Mr. Monk series, and subtitles on anything I watch

Listen: Maroon5, Vance Joy, EDM, Coldplay, Matt Maeson, The Score, Sugar Ray

Watch: The Office, Blue Planet, American President, Good Will Hunting, Miss Congeniality, PBS NOVA, Breaking Bad

Name one thing you are looking forward to experiencing at Stanford.

A hub for vibrant conversations, (generally) warm weather, and opportunities in fields I've never imagined existed. This represents such a stark contrast from where I live now, but it's a change I'm so looking forward to.

Imagine you had an extra hour in the day—how would you spend that time?

My house is like a revolving door—no one ever seems to be home at the same time. An extra hour would offer time to pause and eat dinner as a family, with my parents laughing over rice bowls while my sister and I choreograph Pocketful of Sunshine.

Briefly elaborate on one of your extracurricular activities or work experiences.

No matter how hard I train, I will never win my 200-meter race. But as competitive as I am in the rest of my life, this surprisingly doesn't bother me.

At track meets, I fly as my spikes dig into the soft rubber, propelling me forward. Everything melts away—there are no thoughts, no sounds. Left, right, I sprint down the straightaway. My lungs begin to burn. I press on, pushing myself to the limit. The finish line approaches and I lunge across. Reality rushes back, but the exhilaration remains.

According to Ricky Bobby, "If you ain't first, you're last!" But I guess Ricky Bobby never ran track.

After all, if I followed his logic, I'd be "last" every time I ran. But for me, track is about the thrill of the race, knowing that as long as I give it my all, I can never truly lose.

Reader 1

"SPIV: Clear demonstration of character, growth, change over time

POE: ISEF Best of Category rare for this region. Strong candidate with clear dedication to her research.

Decent writing, IV-2.

Very strong interview—summary: She appears to have an understated organic confidence without boasting. Is very mature both intellectually and socially for her age. Strong personal character and motivated to learn.

PQs: could be hyper-focused, but is involved in many other activities so do not consider it a concern. "

Reader 2

Agree with reader 1 on all points. Shows obvious interest in the sciences and pursuit for knowledge. Note significant challenge, historical moment, IVE.

Reader 1 Scores	
Metric	**Score**
Test Rtg	1
HSR	3
Support	2
EC	1
SP-IV	2
Eval	2
Int	1

Reader 2 Scores	
Metric	**Score**
Test Rtg	1
HSR	3
Support	2
EC	1
SP-IV	2
Eval	2
Int	1

Profile IV

Indiana

Personal Essay

Any sufficiently advanced technology is indistinguishable from magic.

Arthur C. Clarke

Let's talk about computers for a minute. I'm typing this essay on Google Docs, a website located in California that I can access within seconds from my home in Indianapolis. My computer creates a request to send to Google's servers. This request is sent, piece by piece, between dozens of different devices and servers until it reaches its destination. The server responds to my request with what appears to be random gibberish. This message is broken up into pieces and sent, again, across the country in the most efficient route at the instant of sending. As each piece arrives at my home, my computer knows how to assemble these pieces and then interpret the gibberish to display the Google Docs website. Each of us goes through this process hundreds of times each day. We can send information around the world, free of transmission errors, in a fraction of a second. That seems a heck of a lot like magic to me!

The distinction between science and magic, however, can be simplified to one rule: science is reproducible. Magic isn't. Given the right resources and enough time, I could design and build my own computer, my own programming language, my own website. But there is no way that I could learn how to cast the Patronus charm. Maybe Harry can do it, but I sure can't, despite my best efforts.

As a kid, I wanted to be a wizard. Those dreams were cruelly destroyed by the laws of physics. But a young me saw the next best thing: technology. I became determined to learn absolutely everything about my dad's laptop, my mom's iPhone, and my sisters' favorite game: Club Penguin. Our family computer transformed, in my mind, from a magic box to my own approximation of Hogwarts; from something I didn't understand to a place where I could learn the extraordinary. I read articles and watched videos and began to create my own magic. I quickly progressed from a simple "Hello World!" to writing a program to conjugate Latin verbs.

I found computer science is utterly captivating. Much like the math and science classes I loved at school, there were many rules to follow and techniques to arrive at the right answer. Just like the books that I read voraciously, creativity was essential to success. Programming became a tool which I could use to turn my ideas into something real. Anything I could think of, no matter how big or complex, I could build myself, with a little help from my friend Google.

At the age of 13, I fell in love with my own kind of magic, and I've never looked back. Computer science is beautiful because it turns the inexplicable into the explainable. Understanding how something as basic as magnetism can be manipulated and layered to create results as complex and varied as artificial intelligence and spaceships leaves me in awe of the extraordinary combination of the elegance of the physical universe and the miracle of human consciousness.

Intellectual Vitality

I was 13 and bored, looking for something to watch on Netflix. On a whim, I chose Doctor Who, a show recommended to me by my dad. The British accents were a bit off-putting, the special effects comical, but I was blown away. I could feel the couch under my legs and the blanket clutched in my hands, but all I could see was the Doctor and his adventures. He was so clever, able to defeat his enemies with a plan, not a weapon; he was funny, able to reassure people in times of crisis; most outstanding to me, he was full of wonder and a sense of adventure. The Doctor managed to put into words a feeling I have known my whole life: There is so, so much to see.

The world is full of books to be read and music to be enjoyed and people from all walks of life to meet. There are foods to taste and languages to learn and landmarks to take touristy pictures at. There are problems waiting to be solved, people in need of help, a lifetime of sunsets ready to be admired. You can never know everything, but there are so many options: airplanes? Computers? Electromagnetism? Psychology? Political science? I want as much knowledge as I can get.

If Doctor Who has taught me anything, it's to stop waiting and run. Run and see this wonderful world.

Roommate Essay

People are like matryoshka dolls: on the inside, there's a whole other person.

On the outside, I love being alive. I love the world and being in it. I want to see and learn everything. I want to meet all the interesting people in the world, visit all the cool places, learn every language, and experience the full gamut of emotions available to humans. I want to go to the Moon and see the Earth from above, I want to learn the fundamental laws of nature, and find out why everything exists in the first place. I want the full experience.

But on the inside, sometimes, I am empty. I isolate myself, drowning in a pool of emotions and self-destruction. On the inside, I'm just trying to get through the day. There are scars on my skin, more than I can count, from moments when I was absolutely, completely hopeless.

Future Roommate, know this: sometimes I am quiet. Sometimes I just stop in the middle of a laugh. You'll ask, "you okay?" I'll reply, "just tired." Know this: I need distractions. I need hope. I need shelter from reality. I need to not feel numb. I'll listen to happy music and talk to those who love me and I'll feel better.

My two selves coexist. For years, I felt like falling apart. Now, I see my scars, I look up to the stars, and I know that somehow, impossibly, in spite of all my hopeless moments—I am okay.

What is Meaningful to You?

Taken during the Apollo 8 mission, Earthrise is described as "the most influential environmental photograph ever taken."

Most of the picture is black, devoid of life. However, there is a handful of stars, small as specks of dust, billions and billions of miles away and shining for millions of years before the light reaches the camera. The Moon's surface is dusty grey, covered in lumps, bumps, and potholes and so very, very barren. And in the center, a planet reflects bright white and brilliant blue. The clouds, continents, and oceans provide color to the photo, shining brighter than any star. This is a picture of the Earth, the inky darkness merely background, because the Earth is what fills the void. The Earth gives meaning to the universe; the Earth makes the Moon more significant than a big rock and makes the stars more than balls of burning gas. The Earth holds life and will explore and colonize the galaxy.

Where there is life, there is hope; people can do the impossible. The world is full of problems, but I have faith in humanity's ability to make it a better place. I believe that one day humans will master the laws of nature, using science to ensure a paradisiacal life for everyone.

The stars, the vacuum, the Moon are neither good nor evil. They do not care about life or justice or contentment. But that doesn't mean the universe is meaningless. "There is light in the world, and it is us."

What is the most significant challenge that society faces today?

Divisiveness has polarized us. It's us versus them. Anything that hurts them helps us. You cannot question your own side because it strengthens the opposition. Winning becomes more important than being right. Having a civil conversation seems out of reach. Logic and reason give way to blind tribal loyalty.

How did you spend your last two summers?

Last summer, I worked on computer-related projects, traveled for college visits, and fixed a telescope. I also enjoyed a movie-cation with my best friend. The previous summer, I discovered an appreciation for architecture during visits to Fallingwater and the National Building Museum in Washington, D.C.

What historical moment or event do you wish you could have witnessed?

I missed the era of astronauts and space shuttles. I would have been one of those obsessed kids who knows everything about each astronaut and all of their missions and clips all the newspaper articles. My mom watched the moon landing which BLOWS MY MIND.

What five words best describe you?

Enthusiastic, curious, goofy, empathetic, awestruck

When the choice is yours, what do you read, listen to, or watch?

I watch Doctor Who. And read about it. And listen to the soundtracks. I also like to read about computers and space and psychology and political science and science fiction and murder mysteries and detective stories and lots and lots of fanfiction. But mostly Doctor Who.

Name one thing you are looking forward to experiencing at Stanford.

Fountains! I have a deep love of aquatic sculptures, but fear fish and drowning. Fountains are ideal as I am unlikely to drown. Also, California is hot, so I'll dry quickly and won't catch pneumonia and die, like William Henry Harrison. That would be a bummer.

Imagine you had an extra hour in the day—how would you spend that time?

What are the restrictions? Does everyone get an hour or just me? Is it a solid hour or can I break it up? Can I stop time? Are there consequences? What about gravity and other laws of nature—still working? This question has far too many possibilities.

More realistically: sleep.

Reader 1

RM: struggles w/ isolation noted

XHR: great response

Reader 2

PE: writing capable of transporting reader between science and magic. [NAME] pulls evidence from either world to shed light and depth on the other

RM: expresses inner isolation and occasional emptiness (DOFT check)

Stanford essay — fountains

XR — the questions that brings up

Reader 1 Scores	
Metric	**Score**
Test Rtg	1
HSR	2
Support	2
EC	3+
SP-IV	2
Eval	2

Reader 2 Scores	
Metric	**Score**
Test Rtg	1
HSR	2
Support	2
EC	3
SP-IV	2
Eval	2

Profile V

Colorado

Personal Essay

When she gave me a confused, blank stare, I knew that she didn't understand the language that I was speaking. I realized that my job in that moment was not to just understand this subject, but to understand it so well that I could break it into fundamental concepts and explain it to someone who doesn't. I was teaching her the language of mathematics. And it wasn't enough to know it; In order to teach it, I had to master it.

A year and a half ago, I started working as an instructor at Mathnasium Learning Center in Castle Rock. What started as a way for me to make some extra money would quickly become the job that would change my life. This experience was meaningful to me because from it, I realized two things: First, I want to become fluent in the language of mathematics, and second, I want to teach it.

In this moment, I could tell that my young student wanted to give up. We had been learning and reviewing graphs for weeks. A concept that I took for granted, she dreaded each lesson. She asked why graphs have negative values and why some values have a zero in them. I realized that the problem was not her ability to understand. The problem was my ability to translate. In order to be effective, I had to recognize that math isn't just numbers and equations, nor is it simply lines, symbols, and facts. Math is pictures. Math is words. Math is motion. Math is shapes and three dimensions. In order to explain graphing to this particular student, I had to go back to explaining it in a way she could understand. How can I translate it so that it makes more sense?

I needed a new approach. I reminded myself: this student is a visual learner. She needs colors and shapes to help her visualize concepts. So I grabbed paper, markers, and colored pencils, and began to draw a picture for my student. I sketched a graph with a farm, and she was in the middle. There were vegetables in the ground, birds and clouds in the sky, and plants on the x-axis. These objects I drew would help her put the meaning of areas of the graph into context. It was a language she understood.

I started showing her what the values of the coordinate pairs meant in this situation. I asked her about the coordinate (2,-6). Would it make sense for this point to be a cloud or a potato? What about the numbers makes you think one way or the other?

We continued discussions like these and I could see the change in her attitude towards graphing because of the look in her eyes. She was finally starting to understand. It was such a good feeling for the both of us. By translating this idea into tangible and simple ideas,I was able to help her make that crucial connection.

For the following months, my focus in teaching shifted. My number one priority was finding an approach for each and every student that made sense to them. This was a challenge, but it was also exciting for me. I taught myself to look at mathematics in abstract ways. I developed new ways to translate multiplication, fractions, ratios, algebra, and even calculus. Developing new and creative ways of explaining this language helped my students to be successful in math. I enjoy working at Mathnasium because I never run out of topics and ideas to teach. I believe that one of the most important parts about mastering the language of mathematics is the ability to explore fundamentals from a new perspective, and to be open to exploring a concept over and over again. This work experience impacted my perception of mathematics, and inspired me to pursue it professionally. Challenge accepted.

Intellectual Vitality

I've been a math geek for as long as I can remember. However, it wasn't until I took Calculus III at University of Colorado Colorado Springs that I experienced an insatiable hunger to understand math at a deeper level.

A couple of weeks into the course, we learned about Clairaut's theorem, which states that mixed derivatives from the same function are equal, regardless of their order. The concept intrigued me. As the professor spoke, I tested equation after equation in my notes and was astonished. They all supported the theorem!

This, honestly, blew my mind and hooked my imagination. The next day, we covered three dimensional limits. The more my professor explained it, the more fascinated I became. The math made complete sense. It was like a language I could feel.

It was during that week of class that I felt like I was suitable for "My Strange Addiction". I became passionate about mathematical theories. Not only did I want to learn more, I needed to. In the months following, I immersed myself in videos about these ground-breaking ideas. I explored a variety of abstractions from Euler's formula to the math behind a Rubik's cube. I was, and continue to be, empowered by the immensity of mathematics. Sadly, many people never experience this kind of self discovery, but I am grateful that I did. It is truly fulfilling to recognize one's passion, and to have a desire to learn everything about it realizing that it will never be boring.

Roommate Essay

Dear Future Roommate,

How the heck did we get in?!

No really. We need to talk. I can't believe I'm here! It's going to be a great year.

For starters, I can guarantee there will always be root beer in our mini fridge. One of my hobbies is tasting locally brewed root beers when I travel. My favorite was made in New Orleans, and was served at a small cafe. However, since it's hard to get my hands on the more exotic types, I usually settle for Barq's.

In addition, the room will likely be all yours on Sundays and Mondays. One of my goals when I get to Stanford is to join the Debate team. As a result, I will likely be competing on those days. Speech and Debate was one of my favorite activities in high school, and I'm determined to continue it in college.

Also, I enjoy listening to music. Lots of it. But no worries—I use earbuds! The genre I enjoy most is world music. Wait! Don't run away! By that I mean songs sung in Spanish, French, and German. Though I typically don't understand the lyrics, and can hardly pronounce the words, I feel enriched by sounds and rhythms from around the world. Besides, one shouldn't limit themselves in the arts.

Lastly, I can't wait to meet you. We're in for a year of transitions, new people, enlightenment, and lots of studying... and I wouldn't want it any other way. See you soon!

What is Meaningful to You?

The dollar store staff know me as "the girl who buys lots of poster boards". But they're not for science projects, nor for "promposals". They're for protesting. Civic action is something that is meaningful to me. Since I'm not old enough to vote, I choose to march instead. It's become my way of being politically involved.

I didn't start becoming an activist until I was in high school. After being on the debate team and taking AP Human Geography, my political awareness was elevated to a new level. I began to understand more about current events and the complexities of social issues. As I began to develop political opinions of my own, I became more interested in expressing my voice, and I did so at marches and rallies.

I was captivated after my first one. It is energizing to be surrounded by others who are as passionate about an issue as I am. From women's marches, to science marches, to the March

For Our Lives, I felt like I had a voice and had to use it. Emotions varied at these marches, but we all spoke with a unified voice. Silence was not an option.

Civic action is so important to me that I wrote a speech about it my junior year for Speech and Debate, and then competed with it at State! Spreading the word about how important it is to participate in politics (regardless of your belief) was paramount. A voice, if kept silent, is wasted.

What is the most significant challenge that society faces today?

This is GARBAGE. The paper, screen, or computer upon which this essay is read will inevitably become waste. This is THE challenge. It is imperative to develop an effective, global waste management system... soon. Otherwise the byproducts of our human existence will surpass the Earth's capacity to absorb it.

How did you spend your last two summers?

My last two summers were spent strategically: I augmented my studies and padded my bank account. I took two college courses at UC-Colorado Springs (Calculus III and Physics III) while working as a shift lead at Sonic Drive-In and as an Instructor at Mathnasium. I loved every minute of it.

What historical moment or event do you wish you could have witnessed?

A great misfortune is to be alive during an event, but too young to comprehend it. If I could witness a historic moment,

I'd choose the day before 9/11, so that I could behold the iconic Twin Towers and comprehend the magnitude of loss felt... when they collapsed.

What five words best describe you?

"What she wants, she earns"

When the choice is yours, what do you read, listen to, or watch?

When the choice is mine, I love watching Sunday football with my family. The smell of chili, the warmth of my lucky sweatshirt, the family cheers, and our dogs wearing orange Bronco jerseys are unforgettable experiences that I will miss when I start school at Stanford next Fall.

Name one thing you are looking forward to experiencing at Stanford.

I CANNOT wait to graduate from Stanford! I will conquer challenges and build character while learning from and alongside the world's finest scholars. This knowledge will ensure I'm equipped to make a difference in the fields of mathematics and science. Graduation won't be the end ... it will be my beginning.

Imagine you had an extra hour in the day—how would you spend that time?

Neat! With an extra hour in the day, I would spend it with my socks off, on a mat, eyes closed, with hands at heart-center.

Yoga has become my favorite way to relieve stress and focus on my wellbeing. It is good for my health and nurtures my soul. Namaste.

Elaborate on an EC

Glossophobia is the term for a "fear of public speaking". Though 200 million people suffer from it … I most certainly DON'T. On the contrary, I adore public speaking. I discovered Speech and Debate during my Freshman year and I have been on the team since.

Undoubtedly, it is my favorite extracurricular activity in high school. I held an officer position during all four years on the team. For the first three years, I was the Historian. My duties included marketing activities such as creating fundraiser ads, completely redesigning our website, and archiving the team's awards after each tournament. I've been the Interpretation Lead for the last three years. In this role, I am a coach, mentor, and manager to my fellow teammates who also compete in Interpretation Events. I aspire to be an active member of the Stanford Debate team and to continue competing in college.

Reader 1

I seem very enthusiastic and socially minded. Well crafted writing, clear, and witty. Confidence in opinion. Enjoyed essays. SP is great and shines through app. IV is strong and focuses on math. *some redacted stuff*. Demonstrates strong non cogs and multiples POE's. Especially impressed by drive to University of Colorado- Colorado Springs. *redacted stuff*. Leaning in for admit.

PE: Learning how to efficiently teach math, great analysis of math as a language

MS- Haven't seen this style of delivery yet

IV- Math

RM- Seems like she'd be fun

SM- Civic action, activist in high school, "a voice, if kept silent, is wasted".

Reader 2

Agree with reader 1. Bumped her down to 2- as she as not as compelling as others with 2', but no doubt she'll be an excellent addition. In addition to reader 1, *redacted stuff. so sus*. She will thrive and take advantage of opportunities here. Works year round at Sonic, founded physics club, light/standard to our pool otherwise.

PE: Complex thinker, teacher

IV: Strong drive for math

RE: Genuine, quirky, and warm; civic action

Tags

DIV, REL

Reader 1 Scores	
Metric	**Score**
Test Rtg	3
HSR	3
Support	2
EC	1
SP-IV	2
Eval	2

Reader 2 Scores	
Metric	**Score**
Test Rtg	3
HSR	3
Support	2
EC	1
SP-IV	2
Eval	2-

Profile VI

Washington

Personal Essay

For as long as I can remember, I have always enjoyed helping others. Whether it is to edit an English essay or to clarify a chemistry concept, knowing that I have increased my peers' knowledge brings me so much satisfaction. However, I was best at teaching Mandarin Chinese. Having studied Chinese for almost 15 years, I had fallen in love with the rich culture and intricate calligraphy and wanted others to love the language the way I do.

It took me years for me to truly grasp such a difficult language, especially when my family did not speak the language. When my friends signed up for Mandarin Chinese in high school, they also found it to be interesting but very challenging. Most of my peers had the same concerns and struggles about Chinese: they did not understand the different Chinese tone markings and how to correctly write Chinese characters. As the year progressed, more and more people asked me for tutoring help. However, I did not have an organized and simple way to reach everyone and help them succeed in learning the language.

As a result, I began to look for a more accessible way to help as many people who were passionate and curious about learning the language. I began to self-teach how to code and create user-friendly interfaces. As a language tutor, I knew that learning a new language was hard and HTML and C++ were no exception. The skills needed to run a website are equivalent to the skills necessary for speaking Chinese; they need to be perfect in order to be coherent. From that point forward, I spent every night practicing coding problems and running my own programs to ensure that my website would run smoothly.

Even though I stayed up late working on this project, those late nights were worth it. PerfectChinese, my tutoring and resource company, launched six months later. The website now contains a four-year curriculum with textbook dialogues with English translations and is accompanied by authentic recordings. Every chapter corresponds with a vocabulary list, which has important phrases related to each unit and a link to our tutoring page, where students can set up appointments with my tutoring team, and all proceeds benefit our high school's Chinese club.

PerfectChinese's program and website have allowed my peers to easily connect with tutors and access these resources anytime, anywhere. The website has also benefited my school's Chinese program. Now, my school's Chinese teacher begins all her classes by going onto my website, PerfectChinese.org, to listen to recordings and playing vocabulary games. Realizing how much the company has helped students, I am currently developing an app based on it, which will make studying Chinese even more interactive and accommodating to even the most novice learners. Because of PerfectChinese, I have not only learned how to code and apply business tactics, I have also realized that helping others has and will always be a goal of mine.

Intellectual Vitality

When I was six years old, my mom took me to the local Barnes and Noble and let me buy any book I wanted. Being the typical six-year-old girl whose favorite color is pink, I ran over to the history section and picked up a pastel pink book, which happened to be a biography about Amelia Earhart.

After my mom bought me that biography, I rushed home and read through the book that same day. I was so intrigued by how Earhart was able to break gender barriers. Earhart made the six-year-old me realize that women can accomplish anything they put their heart into. I was so mesmerized by this story, I went back to the same section at Barnes and Noble and bought another book about the Revolutionary War. This happened every week for the next seven years. By then, I had amassed a collection with over 200 history books.

My friends think I'm "boring" for spending my weekends curled up in my bed reading a historical novel. But they don't understand the impact history has had on me. Ever since I bought that pink book, I have always been seeking to absorb more than I'm given. In history, whether it's a mistake or triumph, every event has a takeaway and has taught me lessons I wouldn't have learned anywhere else. From watching a documentary on the Civil War to actually visiting a battle site, everything about history excites me and inspires me to continue to learn more.

Roommate Essay

Dear Future Roommate,

My name is [NAME], but my best friends call me [NAME]. I might hug you like crazy but don't worry—I'm just excited to meet you! Future roommate, here are a couple things you should know about me:

I am a foodie. When I'm not watching Buzzfeed's "Worth It" or scrolling through Yelp trying to find the best restaurants, I'm usually trying new dishes for my food blog and spending time with my favorite people. From trying new juice cleanses at the nearby Pressed Juicery to pigging out at Coupa Cafe, count me in for any "foodventure."

I am a photographer— but not your traditional kind. I don't take pictures of the sunset and ocean views, I capture all of life's moments. Yes, I'm that one friend who takes 300 pictures within two hours and creates shared albums with everyone. Even though my friends get annoyed with me (sometimes), I love preserving the fun and unforgettable memories. From getting ready for our first college party to preparing for fountain hopping, you bet I'll be snapping away.

Even though we don't know each other yet, I feel like we are destined to be best of friends. Out of the billions of the people on this planet, we were put together in the same dorm for a reason. From jamming to new bops at the CoHo or pulling all-nighters together, I can't wait to start the craziest adventure of my life with you.

All the love,

[NAME]

What is Meaningful to You?

His name is Fox. He is always supporting me in every way he possibly can. I first met him when I was in middle school— it was love at first sight. I knew we were made for each other. I couldn't stop talking about him, as I gushed about him to my friends and begged my parents to let me have him. Finally, the week before my first day of high school, I saved up my allowance and bought Fox, my Fjallraven (Arctic Fox) backpack. Three years and countless hikes later, Fox and I are still going strong.

In his front pocket, I have my bus pass and wallet: my passports to the world. On the other side, I have my phone and portable charger: the tools needed to survive in today's modern world. There's also a little hole on Fox's head, where I keep my earbuds, which always calms me in the most stressful times. In another compartment, I keep my laptop. Whether I'm finishing a new code or scouring Reddit threads, I am never bored. But Fox's biggest compartment is stuffed with my schoolwork. To many, Fox's stacks of papers, folders, and notebooks like a heavy burden. But for me, this mountain of homework reminds me of school, a hike that lasts seemingly forever.

Even though the trail of life can be bumpy, I still trudge on— learning, growing, and thriving. And I cannot think of a better companion to accompany me on this journey than Fox.

What is the most significant challenge that society faces today?

I read an article written by a computer science professor about why women don't code and cited boys are "just better" at math and science than girls. Society supports these kinds of these untrue stereotypes and whether it's about race or gender, these viewpoints should no longer be accepted.

How did you spend your last two summers?

My summers have been jampacked. Last summer, I traveled to Bangkok and Singapore. Then, I launched PerfectChinese.org and started volunteering at my local hospital. This summer, I studied Java, wrote my research paper about "The Help", and discovered my newfound love for vlogging.

What historical moment or event do you wish you could have witnessed?

I wish I could've witnessed the Red Guards attacking the Four Olds. After writing a research paper on the subject, I realized how much ancient Chinese history was destroyed. To stop them and show them how valuable it is to appreciate our ancestors and history would be a life-changing opportunity.

What five words best describe you?

Determined, passionate, humorous, ambitious, hardworking

When the choice is yours, what do you read, listen to, or watch?

East of Eden—From the characters to Steinbeck's word choice, every detail contributes to this masterpiece

Anything by ABBA—Their tunes always put a smile on my face

Third Rock From The Sun—Every hilarious episode points out the "normal" antics that humans do on a daily basis

Name one thing you are looking forward to experiencing at Stanford.

I can't wait to join Stanford's Student Artificial Intelligence Group. I have always been interested in the way technology is benefiting our community. It would be so worthwhile to use Stanford's state-of-the-art equipment and shape the future with my peers and world-renowned mentors.

Imagine you had an extra hour in the day—how would you spend that time?

25 hours per day? If there really was an extra hour, the world would be chaos. With the ecosystem turning upside down and Earth practically engulfed in flames, I would spend that 25th-hour building a rocket ship so I could move to Mars and get away from this mayhem.

Reader 1

CAPE on creating a website, self-initiation

Pops give insight into CS, IVE doesn't show IV but focuses on love for history

Earnest personality as seen through RME

WME talks about backpack "I trudge on, learning, growing, and thriving"

Would take advantage of SU curriculum

"Yes, leaning in"

Reader 2

Academics and testing strong, Calculus @ Jr. College, Consistent grades

EC [PerfectChinese] initiated and created, the idea to completion

SU meets needs to explore it all

"I agree, leaning in"

Reader 1 Scores	
Metric	**Score**
Test Rtg	2
HSR	3
Support	1+
EC	3
SP-IV	3
Eval	2
Int	2

Reader 2 Scores	
Metric	**Score**
Test Rtg	2
HSR	3
Support	1
EC	2
SP-IV	3
Eval	2
Int	2

Cultural Catalysts

Profile I

Texas

Personal Essay

Every Friday afternoon, my parents and I sell tacos to those who want to taste real tacos. We are entrepreneurs.

Starting the night before service we place our collective minds on the art of the taco.

Good tacos are styled with the Mexican flag of salsas–a fiery green pure serrano pepper salsa, and a burning red tomatillo jalapeño red salsa. Better tacos are those whose steak has been soaking in a bath of lemon-lime juice and salt overnight so that every bite fills your mouth with flavor. But the best tacos–our tacos–come on plates with extra onions and cilantro and limes and jalapeños that we picked for their potential and good looks. Even the less pretty picks seem to take on a new life in the hands of my mother and sister, as they cut and dice and slice them into containers.

My father and I have the honor of chopping the long slices of steak into tiny pinchable squares. We stand shoulder to shoulder with huge chopping knives in our hands. For forty-five minutes—trust me, we've timed it—we both thud away at chopping blocks of wood worn into a dent created by a year of cutting steak. My mother is next to our station precooking twenty pounds of meat. My sister is in the kitchen blending up all the chile for the half-gallon containers. The entire house smells of cooking lemon-lime juice and onion, an aroma of a typical Mexican taqueria.

Around six in the afternoon on Friday, as summer heat dies down and the sun sets, our first customers arrive. Our quadrants of tables are set up, my dad is finishing grilling the onion, my mom is stacking plates and passing out gloves, my sister is sorting and opening all the condiments, and I have a new notepad and pen. A year ago, the first customers would be our family members that were already familiar with my dad's grill skills. Today, it is a family of 4; the man says he heard of us through a friend (who had also been recommended by another friend). I am the greeter, the waiter, the middleman that seals the deal. I am the voice for our business.

"Good afternoon! What can I get for you? We have steak, pork, and stomach".

"Would you like a chile toreado [pressed, rolled, and grilled jalapeño] with that?"

"Your total is twenty-four. Thank you, have a great night!"

I am the voice for our business.

My family and I are dreaming the American Dream. My parents arrived in America with their hopes encapsulated into two kids. They were leaving behind a culture that passes down the life of a homebound wife and hard laboring husband. My grandparents testify to this, and their grandparents do, too. Instead, my parents sought out the land of the free and twenty years later, she is cleaning houses, he is shipping wood stacks across the nation, and we are selling tacos on the weekends. A year ago we sold tacos because my mother had medical bills to pay.

Eight months ago we sold because my sister had room and board to pay. As of four months ago, we sold because we have a food truck to condition with a grill. Today we sell because my dad wants to stop working in a labor-intensive job. I work for them, free of charge because I know that when the time comes around, they will pull their heart and soul, like they do every Friday, into helping my sister and I as we pursue the education they could never receive.

Twenty years ago they left their town of Rio Bravo, Tamaulipas behind, but they brought with them the inherited art of the Mexican taco. Spicy with a taste of lime, our food is made right out of our kitchen and our hearts. We serve every plate with pride.

Intellectual Vitality

I want to be a part of the next age of invention. I read about the age of inventors in the Industrial Revolution in history class and then in art I learn about Rube Goldberg machines, and I think to myself, 'Now THAT's what I want to do with my life.' With silly prototypes or flying cars or 3D interactive displays, with an art and math intensive schedule, I want to create.

I think our civilization is just picking up momentum and we still have room to grow. I want to learn how to materialize my ideas or be a part of a group of students with a similar mind-set. I have a fascination towards cameras and the seemingly abstract idea of turning light into digital files. And I feel there's still so much room for the digital industry to progress. There's the standard representation of the future in the film industry of neon-glowing cities with massive projections of advertisement like in Blade Runner or Ghost in the Shell. Wouldn't real life technology like this make our society that more visually interesting and inspiring? Boolean Algebra is teaching me circuitry and soon enough we will begin learning about clocking LED lights to display numbers. Studio Art is teaching me to turn a concept for a photo into a fully flashy photoshoot. I have the creative background to not be intimidated by a new project. I want to belong to the team of engineers that make the future exciting without losing the passion for the aesthetic. Maybe it's the artist in me or the STEM student in me, but that's what we are taught to think. We are the creators of our own future after all, right?

Roommate Essay

Dear Roommate,

Foremost I should let you know I hang a 3'x5' Mexican flag and an American flag in my room. Along with the flags, I also proudly bring my Mexican culture of playing Spanish music on cleaning days (and I like maintaining a clean area in case of any visitors), and keeping a cross near my bed for divine protection (just as my mother says). I also bring with me a habit of late rising after a good night's celebration, microwave meals, and punk music playing in the background as I lay with my laptop like your typical American boy.

You will probably be able to tell from the plentiful camera equipment I will bring, but my biggest passion is photography, especially fashion shoots. That means I will have a lot of clothes that you can use if you want, and I will also force you to go thrift-shopping with me weekly. I will also be wanting to shoot all the time. You know I'm gonna develop my own line of cameras one some day? Thanks to Professor Wetztein in the Imaging Lab. I'm applying to an as-far-from-Texas school so I can start a new beginning- a beginning with a true sense of my character and without the rooted prejudices of southern etiquette that loom over my county. I want to be more social while here. Don't hold back on introducing me to single girls you know... or single guys.

But we'll talk more once we've settled.

Your roommate,

[NAME]

What is Meaningful to You?

I joined my school's yearbook last year because I saw the opportunity to change a problem of representation in our community. Ask anyone from our district, and they will tell you that Paschal is the whitest school in Fort Worth. My high school is 60% Latinx. Why doesn't it feel like it?

Representation can make a world of a difference to my school. It's bringing to light the existence of groups that do not see themselves in the spotlight, ever. Recently, movies like Moana and Coco are readjusting the spotlight to unnoticed groups. That fills me with much appreciation for creators that use their skills and audience to spotlight people like me. In elementary school, we learned about Jose Hernandez, and my friend wanted to be an astronaut like him. In 2008, I watched Obama's inauguration, and I saw a future of politics with people of color creating a voice for my family. Today RuPaul's Drag Race has national attention, but more importantly, it humanizes the LGBT community. I see a nation that will slowly but surely integrate this minority group into the mainstream and I will feel accepted.

In our Yearbook, I made sure I got many pictures of our star athletes making it to state competitions, our award-winning artists, our dedicated dance team, and our students dressing up for spirit week, all of which are primarily students of color. I am adding color to a book full of white pages. I believe representation matters.

What is the most significant challenge that society faces today?

The absence of communication is the challenge. A hate-torn nation stems from the pandemic disease of "us-versus-them". A simple concept to imagine: only "we" matter because "they" aren't "us". Don't you think it would be different if we didn't stop listening when we don't hear what we want to hear?

How did you spend your last two summers?

In the (HS)^2 program in Colorado, I learned about rock climbing, silversmithing and college. This 3-year summer program helped me prepare for my school year STEM classes, while still providing opportunities for outdoor fun. We hiked mountains, toured colleges, experienced dorm life, and built friendships with students from around the nation.

What historical moment or event do you wish you could have witnessed?

I wish I could have witnessed Hillary Clinton's inauguration. Our first female president would have continued the momentum of unprecedented change. I know it didn't really happen like the prompt suggests, but I wish I had. Girls everywhere would have grown up seeing that women can be successful anywhere.

What five words best describe you?

avantgarde, imaginative, adaptive, pictorial, [NAME]

When the choice is yours, what do you read, listen to, or watch?

RuPaul's Drag Race shows the immense creativity of queer culture while simultaneously showing the vulnerability and the selective family aspect of queer men. For music, my favorite genre is pop punk; the fast guitars and drums and pop melodramatic melodies like The Front Bottoms is my go-to on Spotify.

Name one thing you are looking forward to experiencing at Stanford.

My dream job lives in the Stanford Computational Imaging Lab! I have taken pictures for years now, and I dream of producing new cameras or image gadgets. I really want to see Professor Gordon Wetztein's lab. Also, I'm a sucker for cohesive roof tiling.

Imagine you had an extra hour in the day—how would you spend that time?

Every breathing cell in me wants to answer more sleep! But after we've all adjusted clocks, those extra 2.5 minutes-per-hour slowly fade into routine life. Realistically, an hour isn't enough to make world peace, but I could use those minutes to drink my water and properly hydrate.

Reader 1

IVE: next stage of invention

Reader 2

Reader 1 Scores	
Metric	**Score**
Test Rtg	2
HSR	3
Support	3
EC	3
SP-IV	3
Eval	3

Reader 2 Scores	
Metric	**Score**
Test Rtg	2
HSR	3
Support	3
EC	2
SP-IV	2
Eval	2-

Profile II

Tanzania

Personal Essay

Being an African in the 21st Century means redefining my values. It means struggling to find my place in a society straining under the weight of its traditional values and history while it seeks to cope in a drastically developing and changing world. In many ways it also means that as an educated Tanzanian, I am vulnerable to the dilemma and anger that comes with witnessing the social oppression of women, youth and children in Africa.

I first came to define what being an African today means when at the tender age of 15 I lost my childhood best friend. Mwajuma led a mostly tragic life. She lost her mother when we were twelve. She was raped and stopped schooling when we were fourteen. She was forced to marry an older man when we were fifteen. I have not talked to or met Mwajuma since I learned about her marriage, mostly because of how ashamed and powerless I felt when I was faced with the news. I felt hopeless because I could not stand up and convince her father otherwise. I was angry, mostly at myself for not being able to stand up and help my best friend when I for one knew of her dreams to become a doctor. I have met and heard of many other Mwajumas since then, girls who have been a perfect example of the repressive traditions prevalent in rural Tanzania. Each is sadly part of a statistic—examples of the 94% of Tanzanian girls who don't make it to secondary school but end up married, pregnant or employed by their 18th birthday.

Comparatively, my fate has been a different story. Because I excelled in my lower secondary studies, I received a full scholarship to a prestigious International Baccalaureate School in northern Tanzania. At the International School Moshi, unlike my lower secondary school, the emphasis was beyond just academics. The IB curriculum requires satisfactory service, creativity and sports participation to graduate. This was my opportunity to be a force for change and not just a powerless bystander. I joined a group of friends to raise money to pay the school fees of Elizabeth, an orphan, who otherwise would also have been victim of oppressive traditions. I have initiated a relationship between my school and a local vocational training center focused on female school dropouts and child marriage escapees. We frequently gather to teach these girls English communication skills. I have joined the East African Model United Nations as part of the Human Rights and Global Health Committees. In EAMUN I have found the perfect opportunity to expose myself to the critical process of planning and problem solving while also experiencing what it feels like to be a representative of African and Asian women in a global platform like the United Nations. In my own small way, I have found possible solutions to a major problem plaguing Tanzania and many other African countries.

Over the last few years, I have vowed never again to feel powerless and hopeless. In a male-dominated country of fifty-five million people, the grievances of girls like Mwajuma usually go unnoticed. Seemingly insignificant compared to many other problems that face a developing country like Tanzania. This is why I seek a university education in social sciences. So that I could come back to Tanzania and aid in the struggle already begun. I want to fight traditional prejudices that limit female access to education and the economy and expand their opportunities to support themselves and their families. There is a Swahili proverb in Tanzania, "Muelimishe mwanamke, uelimishe jamii nzima", which means educate a woman and you educate the society. I am encouraged by this adage because it recognizes the role of a woman as the backbone of society. She is an important instrument in our societal struggle to find a place in our ever developing and changing world.

Intellectual Vitality

I always suspected I was my physics teacher's favorite student. So I was not even remotely surprised when in the 10th Grade, he asked me to teach the class the next unit on transformers. In that school, the 10th Grade was the highest one and having no access to the internet, my options were limited. I had no senior students to approach and no online videos to consult. But I was genuinely excited to carry out this challenge.

That night, I gathered all the physics books available and sat down to read them. Whenever I could not understand a particular passage, I consulted another book. I had a piece of paper and pen next to me which I used to summarize all the major ideas. Looking back now, I suspect I must have looked mad: three huge physics books on my lap, three open on my desk, and two on the floor next to me. But that didn't cross my mind. I felt accomplished with every major idea and detail

I understood. I felt intellectually independent to be entrusted with the huge task of not only teaching myself but also my 44 classmates a physics concept. The prospect that the knowledge I obtained, I could use to teach other people excited and still excites me. The next day, after I taught everything I knew on transformers, my teacher walked up to me and said that I did the job of a teacher and even went beyond.

Roommate Essay

If you ask me, the most beautiful place in the world is Tanzania. One of our two amusement parks is a safety hazard. Our electricity is a joke. And if you thought you have come across slow internet, think again. But Tanzania is still the most beautiful place to me. It's the people. The people here are always smiling, they are welcoming and trusting. They are warm. So, Hello future roommate! My name is [NAME] and I'm from Tanzania. I smile often. I like to think that I'm warm and welcoming. I'm certain that I'm both very trusting and trustworthy. And I am excited to meet you. I'm very much a comedy type of girl— How I Met Your Mother, That 70s Show, The Simpsons, and Brooklyn Nine-nine, are my all-time favorite shows. I sleep like a log at night, so nothing you could do can wake me up. Apparently, I have an awful taste in music. In my defense, it's not a crime to like a little bit of everything. Rest assured that whatever you like to listen to, I will too. I'll most certainly come across as shy at first, but within a few hours, I'll be cracking you up with my many expressive repetitive stories. I don't mind any question you could have about Africa or Tanzania. I hope you won't mind my questions—I've always loved learning about other people and places. And, I truly can't wait to make Stanford our home together.

What is Meaningful to You?

My reasons for helping people have always been somewhat selfish. I do not provide help just for the thrill of it, but rather because I get something back from doing so. I have never helped someone who gave me money or food or jewellery. But always, the people I help teach me something. For a huge portion of my secondary career, I helped a classmate called Enna with math. I spent weekends and evening studying time with her. Eventually she passed her final exams.

In exchange, she, unwittingly, taught me something even more important. She taught me how to forgive after I witnessed her forgiving her father who had abandoned her. Because of her, I have found no mistake too awful that cannot be forgiven or forgotten. And because of her, my life has been filled with lightness and happiness. I have found that there is always a gem of wisdom or a mine of talent in the people I meet, and I am always humbled when people open up and let me see and learn from their wisdoms and talents. It is for this reason that I always seek to help or be there for the people around me, just so that I can have the honor of being exposed to their experiences and the lessons I will learn from them.

What is the most significant challenge that society faces today?

Ensuring equal access to resources has always been a major challenge in Tanzania. Women here have limited access to education and the economy, and youth have limited access to employment. Without equal access to resources for all groups, Tanzania and the world will never be truly able to develop.

How did you spend your last two summers?

I spent part of this past summer attending a Yale University summer program in the US. The previous summer, I helped out at a local primary school as an accountant and receptionist where I learnt important computer skills. And I went hiking with my father in my tribal home.

What historical moment or event do you wish you could have witnessed?

For my 4,000-word IB Extended Essay, I decided to investigate the death of the UN Secretary General Dag Hammarskjöld who died from a plane crash that no one can explain. I wish I could witness that plane crash and what caused it, to finally solve the 57-year-old mystery.

What five words best describe you?

Trustworthy, resilient, insightful, compelling, ambitious

When the choice is yours, what do you read, listen to, or watch?

Read: By the River Piedra I sat down and wept, The Book Thief, Quora, New York Times, Wired

Watch: Brooklyn Nine-nine, That 70s Show, How I Met Your Mother, Game of Thrones, Clueless, Trevor Noah Listen: J Cole, Kanye West, Frank Sinatra, Don Williams, Kenny Rogers, George Ezra, Janelle Monáe

Name one thing you are looking forward to experiencing at Stanford.

I have never attended a concert before despite my love for music and performances. Because of this, I look forward particularly to attending Frost—the prospect of finally witnessing a live performance, having fun and forming lasting memories with a group of friends.

Imagine you had an extra hour in the day—how would you spend that time?

Usually long past midnight when I'm done with all my IB course requirements and homework for the day, I'm always so exhausted that I pass out immediately. I'd dedicate the extra hour to the one thing I've loved since I was 6—I'd read a book.

Reader 1

On the fence with a gentle lean in for committee consideration— [NAME] is a strong student in a competitive school group sitting at 1 or 2 in her class, which is notable having come from a public TZ school system (little internet, much smaller town, hence RU) in the 11th to the more rigorous IB program. Leadership at school including Head girl.

[NAME]'s writing is warm and engaging: she's a social scientist with a focus on empowering women which is a theme across her essays.

While she may not have the firepower to emerge in this selective pool, the academic prowess is there with some IV starting to develop; she needs a second read given academics and context for TZ.

Reader 2

Lots to like. Academic profile is excellent. 10th exams scored top 2 in the country with incredible journey from rural TZ to ISM on scholarship. Writings are thoughtful, critical and mature. Lean in.

Reader 1 Scores	
Metric	**Score**
Test Rtg	2
HSR	3
Support	3
EC	3
SP-IV	3
Eval	2+

Reader 2 Scores	
Metric	**Score**
Test Rtg	2
HSR	3
Support	3
EC	3
SP-IV	3
Eval	2+

Profile III

Belgium

Personal Essay

If I wrote an autobiography, it would be titled "The great discourse on the importance of identity". Its concluding chapter would be something like this: "Identity, in my personal experience, serves as the fundamental basis of a person's life. It is-effectively- who they are. And who they are becomes what they do".The entire book would encompass my struggle with identity. It would be full of hilarious anecdotes and pretentious language to disguise that fact that my struggle with identity is really none of those things. It is neither hilarious, and hopefully, not pretentious. In fact, it is rooted in simple facts, and events of history that resonate deeply through me.

As a Tibetan who has lived in multiple countries, the importance of identity is not lost on me. Every time someone asks me where I'm from, I have to carefully phrase my answer. My answer almost always begins with an awkward laugh, followed by this exact sentence: "I'm Tibetan". Notice that my answer does not begin with "I'm from..". Because it seems false to claim to be "from" Tibet, having never been there physically. I was born in Pretoria, South Africa. My father claims that I was the first Tibetan girl to have been born in South Africa, although I'm not entirely sure I believe him. Not long after I was born, I was whisked away to Paris, where I would spend the next four years of my life. After that, I was placed in a boarding school in the foothills of the Himalayas, in India. You can see why I have had to regularly introduce myself.

I've lived a very privileged life. I have traveled to several countries, I attend one of the most prestigious boarding schools in India, and I have friends that belong to more faiths and backgrounds than I can imagine. As a second generation refugee, my privilege is made especially clear when comparing my life to my father's. As a young child, he was orphaned by the brutality of the violence that occurred in Tibet. He was forced to flee his country on foot, through the Himalayas to India. As a young child, he was placed at the mercy and generosity of a new, foreign country. Fortunately, India would soon become a home to the both of us.

Throughout all the changes in my life, my identity has remained constant. For me, understanding where I "come" from, my country, has effectively shaped my beliefs. In fact, I am heavily influenced by the often violent and brutal history my people have experienced. It is because of my Buddhist identity that my friends make sure to never kill mosquitos in my presence. It is because of my identity as a Tibetan that I feel compelled to tell everyone I come across about my country; to raise awareness of the gross human rights violations taking place. It is the same reason I aim to serve my people: the underprivileged refugees left at the mercy of foreign institutions, or even my people in Tibet, the oppressed, the defenseless, the desperate. Coming from a Tibetan family, I am constantly reminded of the horrors my people have had to suffer, the thousands that were killed in and out of Tibet, the countless that have set themselves on fire in their desperation. Often times, I feel devoid of hope. I am too young, too inexperienced— a single person unable to better the life of my fellow Tibetans. But my people are resilient; and in turn, it has become a crucial part of my identity. I am determined to help our situation: to spread the privilege and the opportunities that I have been so graciously awarded, to others, to be able to inspire hope in times there are none. I want to do all this because of who I am, but more importantly, who I can be.

Intellectual Vitality

For a school trip senior year, me and around 20 classmates went on five day rafting expedition on the Ganga. We would raft as long daylight permitted and then find a large enough riverbank to camp on at night. Our guide, Promod, was young, sarcastic, and incredibly knowledgeable about all the workings of the Ganga. Prior to this experience, I had little to no interest in river currents or the effects of different natural events on the course of a river, but this trip made me curious. Every time there was a change in the river, Promod would point it out, and carefully explain to all us amateur rafters what it was. It was through this trip that I learned what an eddy current was, or how some dips in the river resembled washing machines and how to avoid them. Being on the river was a refreshing new way of learning, and our proximity to nature made me excited for the next day. It felt good to be able to apply the knowledge our guides had given us to make decision on where to camp for the night or what route to take through rapid. Frankly, it replenished my faith in education. Promod was an excellent teacher and the river was an excellent classroom. And whenever the slightest hint of boredom hit, Promod would be sure to chuck us in the cold water to cure it.

Roommate Essay

Hey roommate,

How are you? Are you excited? Nervous? I know I am. I recently watched a movie about a psychotic girl who tries to kill her college roommate. I guess that doesn't exactly set the best precedent as far as college roommates go. But I assure, I, in no way, resemble that girl. So, I just wanted to tell you a few things about myself to put your mind at ease. I go to boarding school so I've lived in dorms all my life. I watch a lot of horror movies even though they give me nightmares. I like plants, although I'm not very good with them. I come with a supply of ramen noodles because let's be honest, ramen is delicious. On the subject of food, I would like to mention that Tibetan food is fantastic. And if you haven't tried it, we'll rectify that situation immediately. I'm an excellent sleeper, so don't worry about have having the lights on or working late. I have terrible vision in one eye so I wear glasses. Sometimes when I forget, I turn my head one way and squint. It's slightly creepy to be on the receiving end of this look (I've been told), but I'm just trying to focus. One last thing- my current roommate said her favorite thing about me was my habit of folding clothes when I'm stressed. So if you're closet is unorganized, you're in luck.

I'm so excited to see you!

[NAME]

What is Meaningful to You?

Among the clutter of books, stray papers, candles and fake plants on my desk is a single glass jar of soil. It's not really the most aesthetically pleasing of decor, but it serves a symbolic purpose. Over time it's become one of my most valuable possessions. A friend's mother went to Lhasa, Tibet on vacation recently and asked me if I wanted her to bring anything back. I said I wanted some soil. She gave me a slightly quizzical look, but agreed anyway. She understood what soil from Tibet would mean to me. I know, it's incredibly cheesy, but it's the closest I will realistically ever get to home. I wanted something I could physically see everyday to remind myself of where I come from, and where I hope to return one day. I decided that if I couldn't travel to Tibet myself, I could at least have a piece of my home on my desk. My experiences of Tibet come entirely from the stories I was told by my father and my older relatives. I think it is common among second generation Tibetan refugees to feel slightly nostalgic for a country most of us haven't experienced. Despite the fact that I've never experienced Tibet first hand, I always imagine the possibility of going to Tibet as a grand return, of going home. The soil reminds me I am never too far away from that dream.

What is the most significant challenge that society faces today?

Empathy. Somehow, in an age where technology allows us to be so connected, we have become detached from each other. We maintain a terrifying level of apathy to situations that aren't directly relevant to ourselves. Encouraging dialogue that engages different people can help combat this illness.

How did you spend your last two summers?

I spent last summer in Brussels. It was the first time I had seen it sans blanket of snow, so I became a tourist: I visited all the museums, monuments, and tourist attractions. The summer before I spent interning at the Tibet Policy Institute in Dharamsala, working around driven people.

What historical moment or event do you wish you could have witnessed?

The Cuban missile crisis marked time when diplomacy prevailed. The crisis highlighted the impact of an individual, such as Vasili Arkhipov refusing to launch a nuclear torpedo, in saving humanity. I wish I could have experienced the global sigh of relief at the end of the confrontation.

What five words best describe you?

spicy, conscientious, curious, involved, sister

When the choice is yours, what do you read, listen to, or watch?

Read: Any book by Murakami, any kind of comic, books with fairies and/or a sarcastic female lead

Listen: Christmas Music, because it's the closest I get to celebrating Christmas

Watch: Elementary, any house renovation show on the BBC network, brooklyn 99, documentaries about north korea or sea creatures

Name one thing you are looking forward to experiencing at Stanford.

Other than the extraordinary academic programs and the unique activities and traditions at Stanford, I look forward to exploring the Cactus garden. I think it is such a cool feature and I am a big fan of cacti.

Imagine you had an extra hour in the day—how would you spend that time?

I would spend it with my family. I have spent enough time at boarding school to pass up on opportunities to spend time with my family. We could go to a dance class together, although I'm not entirely sure my father would enjoy it. Perhaps taking a painting class together?

Reader 1

soft academics, circumstances of school make extra curriculars difficult

Reader 2

will add to the depth of diversity on campus interesting background and life experience

Reader 1 Scores	
Metric	**Score**
Test Rtg	3
HSR	3+
Support	3
EC	3
SP-IV	3
Eval	3

Reader 2 Scores	
Metric	**Score**
Test Rtg	3
HSR	3-
Support	3
EC	3-
SP-IV	3
Eval	3

Profile IV

Illinois

Personal Essay

As a kid, I would often venture out to the edge of the pond at the end of my street, where the cattails that poked out of the clear water grew thicker and taller until they towered over me into a grassy wetland that seemed to stretch on forever. Then, I would run and run, reeds snapping and crunching beneath my feet, until my house had disappeared completely from view, until the roar of the nearby highway faded into the rustling of tall grasses, until everything was unrecognizable except for the sky above my head. Immersed in the dense grasses, I would become a mischievous runaway, or a lost princess, or an intrepid explorer.

In play, I was shapeshifting, infinite. The prairie belonged to me. But according to the stories repeated all around me, the prairie belonged to the pioneers, heaving with dysentery as they crossed the plains in cramped covered wagons, braving bitter winds, killing turkeys, and fending off dangerous natives, so they could build log cabins and civilize the frontier. What belonged to me had been left behind long before I was born, when my parents immigrated from China. Here, I spoke 'surprisingly good English', was constantly asked for my 'real name' , and listened intently at school as we learned not only about the pioneers, but of a full cast of white men who had discovered the world. Then, we studied the Western canon in English and played European classical music in Orchestra.

On my own time, I read books about mothers who called their daughters 'hon' and watched families say grace before dinner on television. I had no part in these stories. My classmates saw my black hair and almond eyes and deemed me shy and quiet (and good at math) before I even had the chance to open my mouth (or fail a calculus test). I found myself being talked over, pushed past in the halls. I stopped going out to the pond with the cattails.

At home, my parents told me stories about walking barefoot with their siblings to school, great-uncles escaping the Communists in the night, aunts working in re-education camps. I facetimed my grandma at night because she was on the other side of the world. We recited ancient poems about full moons and faraway homes. I debated my mother, argued with my sister, yelled about my hopes and dreams. But at school, surrounded by white classmates, I succumbed to the gap in the story. My every action boiled down to enforcing or defying a stereotype, and I strained to fit within this dichotomy. Despite the expansive grasslands we lived in, the limited narratives that existed for Asian people did not grant me enough space to be a full person.

Still, when I thought of home, alongside memories of folding overstuffed dumplings with my family and speaking broken Mandarin, I always remembered the bluestems in the park brushing against my calves, smelled the ash of controlled burns in the fall, felt the soft black soil of my backyard between my toes. I wondered: What if I been told a different story about the prairie?

I began to seek out stories that could expand this limited narrative. I read novels written by people of color. I wrote poems and made art that explored the nuances of my experience. I was able to take a course in which I learned American history through the discussion of multiple perspectives. I joined a club that helped me start conversations with students and faculty about race and inequity. Gradually, I carved out new space that included my voice. Then, I began to reclaim my home. I took long sunset runs through local restorations, planted milkweed with my friends, hiked grassland trails, and knew that no matter what I was told, I was an integral part of this place, and it was an integral part of me.

Intellectual Vitality

While other English teachers lectured and quizzed, Mrs. Forde facilitated dialogic discussion. Desks arranged in a circle, we engaged in class discussion almost daily. After laying the foundation for each discussion through a detailed framework of thought-provoking case studies, open-ended questions, and diverse primary sources, Mrs. Forde rarely spoke: the findings we shared, the claims we supported or refuted, and the conclusions we reached were all up to the students. For the first time, I was excited to participate: Without the teacher's dictation, every student's insights played a crucial role in say, deciphering disjointed narration in the Sound and the Fury or deciding on the morality of war in The Things They Carried.

I also grew more confident: Through constant conversation with my classmates, I came to know them well, and stopped being afraid to speak up because I trusted them to listen and respond without judgement. Because we were all equal players in the quest to find meaning, we recognized the value of each other's voices.

Discussion proved such a powerful way to learn that I began to seek it out wherever I could. I started writing case studies for my tutoring students to discuss, and engaging my young Sunday School charges in group conversation. I applied to Stanford, where I knew I would take discussion based seminars. After realizing that learning could be a continually evolving collaboration between students and teachers to build knowledge, rather than a simple one-way transmission of information, I never wanted to go back.

Roommate Essay

I like working with my hands and running through the woods. I keep my nails short so I can dig into my cello fingerboard, and avoid letting charcoal, clay, and other art/life detritus to gather underneath them and turn my cuticles into hideous swamp monster claws. A vocational survey once recommended I become the driver of a cement mixing truck, but I'm not sure Stanford offers that major. I touch lots of dirt (I'm bringing plants!) and give lots of hugs because they both increase serotonin levels in the brain. Speaking of hugs, if you need me, I'll be there for you. I like to think I give sound advice, and I will never leave you on read.

I promise I'll fight the urge to scribble all over our dorm walls. I'm an artist, and also an anarchist. I regularly fight the Man by cutting bagels into chunks instead of slicing them through the middle, putting the 'R' earbud into my left ear, and refusing to limit my perception of other people by the trappings of their identity. These are vital, but they are never your sole distinguishing features. I will strive to understand you as the full, multitudinous person you are.

I'm excited to meet you! When making art, I start with nothing and simply trust in my ability to make something beautiful. I take the same approach to making friends. So even though I don't know you yet, I trust that we will have a great time together.

What is Meaningful to You?

Every morning, my grandma would sit on a creaky folding chair on the stoop of my house and sip tea from a clunky thermos as she waited for the van that took her to the senior center. Sometimes, she would take naps from midday into the evening and still come out to wait when she woke up, no matter what time it was. Once, I came home late at night, and there she was, in the dark, clutching her thermos in the flimsy chair, quietly waiting for the van to come. In photo albums, she was a little girl hugging a stuffed rabbit, then a woman, laughing as she biked through the city, and then a grandmother, cradling my sister and me. But by the time I was old enough to wonder about the person in the photographs, she'd faded away under years of deafness and progressively worsening Alzheimer's. When she returned to live with us, we struggled to communicate with her, and she, likely overwhelmed by her rapidly decreasing personal agency, seemed to have given up. But my family hadn't: we began sitting down with her and writing her notes. I'd tell my mother something to ask her in broken Chinese. My mother would translate my message more smoothly, scrawl it onto a slip of paper, and show my grandmother, who would squint, read it, smile, and reply. As we patiently pushed through the barriers of language, hearing, and memory, my grandmother was able to tell her stories again.

What is the most significant challenge that society faces today?

Combating polarization. Rather than a fight to prove the other side wrong, a disagreement should be viewed as an opportunity to listen, reevaluate assumptions about the other side, and work towards common understanding. Standing up for one's values is extremely important, but so is understanding perspectives different from one's own.

How did you spend your last two summers?

I went outdoors whenever possible, created new friendships, strengthened old ones, spent time alone, volunteered at bilingual summer camps, performed Bach and Elgar, drove long distances, hung out with my grandma, searched for my artistic voice. I read widely and deeply. I found intrinsic motivation. I grew into myself.

What historical moment or event do you wish you could have witnessed?

I would go back in time to before rapid commercial development turned the dense woods in my area into a suburb, before heavy pest control eliminated the bugs and then the birds in my neighborhood. I would love to witness my town with a balanced ecosystem, fresh air, and birdsong.

What five words best describe you?

irreverent, conscientious, creative, compassionate, in-progress

When the choice is yours, what do you read, listen to, or watch?

For emotionally complex melodies with a metanarrative: Mitski.

For the intersection of music, poetry, and truth: Noname.

For stream of consciousness jazz-hip hop: Sen Morimoto.

For when no one else is around: Disney Channel Original Movie soundtracks

Name one thing you are looking forward to experiencing at Stanford.

The student-led "creative ecosystem" at Stanford's Institute for Diversity in the Arts doesn't exist at any other school. Both in and out of class, I'll be able to collaborate with other artists-scholars, study intersectionality, and cultivate an art practice that advocates for marginalized voices and fosters cultural change.

Imagine you had an extra hour in the day—how would you spend that time?

This time next year, I'll live at school (hopefully at Stanford!), giving me less than a year left as a permanent resident in my home. I would hang out (play Fortnite) with my little sister, talk to my parents, and savor my last few months living full-time with my family.

Reader 1

EC 2, Farf 2. leadership roles, see highlight

SPIV 3

PE shows keen social awareness, SE shows excitement for learning which is appealing

PE: dealing w/ racial stereotypes, sought out different narratives to carve out a space of belonging

Why SU: exact quote of my answer

SE: excited about discussion, values participation and others' voices

WM: heartwarming

Reader 2

energy of someone that is ready to break down stereotypes and have the deep discussions needed today. she is interested in all 3 interested and it is evident in her application

Reader 1 Scores	
Metric	**Score**
Test Rtg	1
HSR	3
Support	2
EC	2
SP-IV	3
Eval	2-
Int	1+

Reader 2 Scores	
Metric	**Score**
Test Rtg	1
HSR	3
Support	2
EC	2
SP-IV	3
Eval	2-
Int	1+

Profile V

California

Personal Essay

Upon arriving to D.C., I felt out of place. A curly-haired, tie-dye-wearing, Colombian, California girl like me didn't quite fit into a boarding school full of blazers and Vineyard Vines.

But it quickly became my home. It wasn't just D.C. or the School for Ethics and Global Leadership (SEGL), but more so the community of 23 other politically-minded juniors—each with a unique background. Our daily routine included theatrically reciting the Saint Crispin's Day speech on the metro ride to school, debating what the US should have done during the Rwandan Genocide, exploring how to harness blockchain technology to prevent illegal deforestation in the Amazon, and occasionally attending a congressional session. But as extraordinary as those opportunities were, my most significant learning experiences came from midnight conversations with my classmates in the dorms.

My peers became my greatest teachers. For Marie, going to boarding school meant she could no longer help her family pay their bills. While inner-city Boston and the Silicon Valley are worlds apart, we found common ground in being daughters of immigrants. Palmer taught me about her experience being lesbian in the Bible Belt, and we shared a love of music, nature, and Vine compilations. Cameron helped me understand the foundations of conservative ideology, and we shared the same dream: to become president of the United States.

One day, after a run along the National Mall, four of my closest friends and I sat in the grass behind the Capitol Building, discussing what our futures might hold. Lillian, always so organized, would be chief of staff, Eunsoo would be a UN ambassador, and Mike an environmental lobbyist. We wondered who could be president. I smiled at my friends and said, "That'll be me."

My roommate, one of the most progressive people I know, tilted her head. "[NAME]—you're kidding if you think America would ever elect a Latina."

In that moment, I felt naive to have seen Obama as proof that anyone could be president. My dream began with him. I remember attentively watching the inauguration in my second-grade classroom. My classmates were talking, doodling, and barely paying attention, but I was invested in every word. Even then, I noticed how Obama strove to understand the perspectives of those who were different from him. His commitment to life-long learning made the impossible possible: after centuries of institutionalized oppression, a black man finally stood where 42 white men previously had. A Latina can do the same.

While my time at SEGL was an immense privilege, the most valuable aspect of that experience is something I strive to incorporate into my everyday life. Like Obama, I have found that connecting with people from drastically different backgrounds broadens my worldview, augments my understanding, and pushes me to reevaluate what I know about myself. Yes, I am

Latina, but my experience as a Latina is different from that of, say, the newly-immigrated students I give high school tours to back home in Mountain View. None of them speak English, few have parents who attended college, and many can barely afford the immunizations required to attend school. Learning from them has helped me recognize the disparities in the Latin American narrative. Similarly, at my job as a receptionist at a boxing studio, I am inspired by my coworkers—a teen mom, an ex-convict battling MS, and an oncologist nurse who survived a stroke. Just listening to their day-to-day stories deepens my knowledge of the nuances of privilege.

My coworkers, the immigrant students at my high school, and my friends from SEGL remind me of why I want to be president. Although I am working against the odds of history, a Latina president is possible, as I am no less qualified than a white man like Cameron. In fact, a great president and citizen should strive to understand the perspectives of all. And in that, I have what it takes.

Intellectual Vitality

I traveled to Rwanda to learn how to forgive. While studying the genocide in school, I was told the country overcame because of forgiveness. But how was forgiveness possible?

Months later, I was in Rwanda, hoping to have my questions answered. With my feet sinking into the mud, I battled the language barrier to ask a convicted perpetrator, "Why did you do it?"

He broke eye contact.

"We had a bad government."

I was unconvinced, and my questions remained unanswered. I conversed with Carl Wilkens, a missionary and the only American to stay during the genocide, questioning the idea that "everything happens for a reason." I was aghast at how other countries perpetuated the tragedy. A journalist told us the least Clinton could have done was acknowledge the genocide—even that would have made a difference.

But I also felt inspired. From watching the first all-women's drumming group to finding beauty in a memorial at a former killing site, Rwanda was breathtaking. Piles of tattered clothes resembled the hilly landscape, and light shining through shrapnel holes evoked the star-filled night sky. This juxtaposition was something I could not experience in a classroom.

In Rwanda, I learned it is possible to come back from anything. More broadly, I witnessed the value of immersive education. History cannot be fully grasped through textbooks—it is best understood by hearing others' stories in person. As a political science major, these experiences are crucial to my education. By embracing discomfort, we learn from those we disagree with.

Roommate Essay

Dear future roommate,

My name is [NAME], but you can call me [NAME]. Here are some things you should know about me:

I think in puns and occasionally speak in hashtags. I'm fluent in four languages: English, Spanish, Spanglish, and meme. You'll likely hear these when I'm on the phone with my parents, who immigrated to California from Colombia but never left their culture behind.

I like to say that I'm a product of science because I was conceived in a petri dish. I attribute my ability to lick my elbow and other superhuman powers to this. But at 12 years old, I was disappointed to discover that I was not, in fact, a demigod. Still, while I may not be the daughter of Poseidon, nothing makes me feel more alive than swimming in the icy Northern California waves. Maybe we can take up surfing together.

I'm definitely a night person—expect to hear my philosophical questions, ethical dilemmas, and startup ideas around 2 am. But there are a few things I'll get up early for, such as kickboxing (the best way to de-stress) and the unparalleled sunrise from Mount Tam. I like to start my mornings by listening to podcasts, drinking yerba mate, and recounting my latest dream.

But enough about me—I want to know about you. What do you love? What would you fight for? Why do you see the world the way you do? We'll have so much to learn from each other.

Your future friend,

[NAME]

What is Meaningful to You?

I come from a country that is often misunderstood. Tucked behind the towering Andes lies a valley home to Bogotá's immense urban sprawl. In the US, whenever I meet another

Colombian, we share an instant bond. Small moments, such as reluctantly eating ajiaco on Sundays to appease grandma, transcend everyone's experience in the community.

Although I did not grow up in Colombia, it has always felt like home to me. I carry pride for my country of origin everywhere I go, regardless of the misconceptions others have. Colombia is so much more than drugs and violence, and the country has demonstrated what it means to turn the tide on history. Now, a pioneer for peace, Colombians are eager for change.

Coming from two places—Colombia and the United States—has helped me understand both sides. I am both the oppressor and the oppressed; the colonizer and the colonized. Even my genetic makeup highlights the intersection of Spanish and indigenous ancestry clashing to form something new. I have learned to see through the lens of a critic, better comprehending the flaws and triumphs of each place I call home while working to improve both. Whether that means standing up for disadvantaged groups in the US or striving to create a more inclusive society in Colombia, both have taught me to prioritize justice.

My dual cultural identity is meaningful to me as it has empowered me to push for growth, both by confronting the issues I witness and learning from my own mistakes.

What is the most significant challenge that society faces today?

Scientists estimate that we have 12 years until the point of no return. Climate change directly threatens both the natural world and the institutions we have created. Corporations, individuals, and governments worldwide must take greater responsibility for their effect on the environment. While sometimes inconvenient, change is necessary.

How did you spend your last two summers?

Worked as a hostess, road-tripped from Boston to DC, attended California Girls State, traveled to Rwanda to learn about the genocide and community reconstruction, visited my sister in New York City where she interned at Facebook, and went to Rangeley, Maine for a reunion with my friends from boarding school.

What historical moment or event do you wish you could have witnessed?

In 1984, Rodrigo Lara, Colombia's former Minister of Justice and my grandmother's cousin, sat before the Colombian legislative house and exposed the political corruption Pablo Escobar and the Narcos had created. Lara was later assassinated; he risked his life for the sake of justice and the betterment of the country.

What five words best describe you?

Spunky, Ambitious, Forthright, Charismatic, Bold

When the choice is yours, what do you read, listen to, or watch?

The New York Times, The New Yorker, The Daily, Fresh Air, documentaries, Drake, Young Thug, Big Sean, Jase Harley,

Jeopardy, classical music, non-fiction books on feminism or race, Vox, contemporary poetry, A Boogie Wit Da Hoodie, Picture Atlantic, The Beatles, Fader, Genius, Stanford Politics, The Mountain View High School Oracle

Name one thing you are looking forward to experiencing at Stanford.

Working as a ticket sales associate for Stanford Athletics has allowed me to experience football games from the outside, but I want to know what it's like when Stanford is my school. I look forward to dancing to "All Right Now" alongside LSJUMB and celebrating the next Big Game win.

Imagine you had an extra hour in the day—how would you spend that time?

I would spend my time hiking with my family. Growing up, we often would hike together, but in recent years, we have grown busier. Hiking would grant me more quality time with my parents, sister, and dog as we enjoy nature—an integral component of my life.

Reader 1

IVE makes great case for IR

WM is self aware

Reader 2

clear depth of IV and PSC

Tags

DIV, SIBL

Reader 1 Scores	
Metric	**Score**
Test Rtg	2
HSR	3
Support	2
EC	3
SP-IV	2
Eval	2

Reader 2 Scores	
Metric	**Score**
Test Rtg	2
HSR	3
Support	2
EC	2
SP-IV	2
Eval	2

Profile VI

Georgia

Personal Essay

Some might say it's emasculating to have a butterfly as a spirit animal. Perhaps I should've gone with the dragon—my Chinese nickname—but the resourceful Viceroy butterfly Limenitis archippus created an identity too relatable to pass up.

I was tricked into learning the viola in 6th grade. The orchestra director distributed lychee jellies to all orchestra students during morning practice sessions. At first, I resisted the temptation, but once she offered mango drops, I caved like Persephone eating the pomegranates. Hades would've been proud; Mrs. McClellan invited me to the viola section (affectionately called music's Underworld) with the enticing nectar, and I, like Persephone, migrated eagerly.

The Underworld turned over a new leaf for the caterpillar to chew on. Complex chord structures. Fast-paced vibratos. Beautiful, drawn-out trills and tensioned octaves overlapping with grace notes. In music, I realized my power to hover between the different flowers of musical styles. Wagner's graceful lulls intertwined with Strauss's angst to create layers for hiding under—worlds of raw emotion and elegance concealed by camouflage; the world I desired to enter the most was the All-State Orchestra.

I didn't make All-State the first year I auditioned, but the emotional bond between music and me compelled me to continue.

The system favored the Monarch caterpillars—wealthy children with European instruments, private instructors, and tiger parents who pushed them into practicing. However, I was just a Viceroy caterpillar unable to afford all of those privileges.

My rejection motivated me to broaden my instrument range. Each of my instruments embodies a part of my personality. Stella, my introverted viola, whispers lullabies, but she sometimes lacks the confidence of the European violas because she suspects that she was cheaper. I rescued Draco the Bass from the storage closet (named for my zodiac and envy of Harry Potter). He had obviously been working part-time shifts after school; although his pegs are worn and he has tic-tac-toe tattoos engraved in his wood, his sarcastic persona sometimes slips a witty tease. Adeline the Piano, named after "Ballade pour Adeline," the first song I practiced improvising on, shares my guilty pleasure of reading rom-com novels. Nicholas the Guitar, although raised Christian, questions society's mandates. He's empathetic and often feels the need to remind me that the Earth and I are not the center of the solar system. Between the five of us, we fluttered between swing jazz, waltzy adagios, and modern pop; our unique voices blended to create musical covers and original compositions. And through this instrumental phase of metamorphosis, I progressed from my caterpillar stage to a chrysalis.

Like the harmless Viceroy butterfly utilizing batesian mimicry and adopting the coloration of the toxic Monarch butterfly, I—through YouTube—copied the idiosyncrasies of the world's best string players. By incessantly pausing and resuming clips, I perceived the slight adjustments these Monarchs made. Bozo

Paradzik favors a stiff left hand and a German bow to force pressure, Rinat Ibragimov tilts the angle of his bowings to slide quick crescendos, and [NAME] drifts through hundreds of their videos. I sorted through dozens of camera angles and hours of tutorials to substitute for the world I wasn't allowed to enter because of cost barriers. Although I envied the pace of metamorphosis of the privileged Monarch pupae, I trusted my mimicry to hold its own.

During the second audition year, I dragged both Stella and Draco to the All-State warm-up room. Draco was up first, and he timidly crawled into the audition room, his frame slouched forward and endpin scraping across the floor.

"Sight-reading excerpt two."

A lyrical piece. Just focus on mixing Rabbath's vibrato with Robinson's tone.

The fourth line of the excerpt climaxed at a high E flat. Fourth position. A difficult pitch to nail, but we've sung this before.

I fluttered through the chromatic scale to reach the note, vibrato-ing the E flat.

Holding the note for ... One.

Two.

Three.

And I sneezed.

I paused, momentarily distracted.

I did what I should've done the second I left my cocoon.

I raised my wings

And I flew.

… Two acceptances and Principal Chair Bassist.

Intellectual Vitality

"Excuse me, do you have any ziploc bags that I could borrow?" I asked the withered coding professor at GHP as I popped into his room at nine P.M., "It's an emergency, and I just saw the biggest boll weevil and I need it for my neuroscience project." Startled, the professor pulled out a most sophisticated tool of capture: a red Solo cup. He handed me the cup, much to the bewilderment of my music major friend who muttered something along the lines of "crazy science majors" as I started spewing facts about the weevil's impressive track record of destroying cotton and its extensive migrational patterns. Unabashed, I scooped up the weevil and placed it within the terrarium that my instructor had lent me.

I first encountered the boll weevil and its other evil associates in the Science Olympiad event Invasive Species. It was one of the events overshadowed by big name events such as Anatomy and Physiology and Thermodynamics, but it was an event that was wholly mine. I put dozens of hours into my thick, three-ringed binder because I loved exploring the disruption of environment that these organisms caused. Joining this event has fostered a love for conservation, and I eventually branched out to compete in other earth science events such as Hydrogeology,

Ecology, Dynamic Planet, and Herpetology. Science Olympiad has made me realize that learning should not be limited to grades; learning encompasses passion and curiosity buried within an ingrained desire to explore the world.

Roommate Essay

Dear roommate,

I'm [NAME], the Korean-Chinese Half-blood Prince from Atlanta who's a prospective environmental engineer.

First of all, I hope you're spiritual (I'm a Southern Baptist) because eventually, I'll convert you to the ever-welcoming religion of Kpop. Postmodern jazz jukebox is also a lifestyle. You'll have an exclusive front-row seat to my off-key sing-alongs when I'm stressed.

I have music nights and grab a few of my instruments (Nick Copernicus the guitar, Stella the viola, Draco the bass, and Adeline the keyboard) to cover pop songs. You'll hear me slamming away on the Chainsmokers or David Guetta. If you have any suggestions, if I can find the sheet music, I can play it.

I keep a stash of Chinese melon lozenges and Kopiko caffeine candies (to eat during class when I start to doze off), and I get them on the down low from a lady in Chinatown, so help yourself whenever. I'm also an environmentalist and will pester you if you ever bring straws into our room.

I hope you like late night talks because I'll be hosting Ramen parties (Shin Ramen. None of those disgusting American imitations) with Aloe vera or Milkiss refreshments. I'm also super into slam poetry, so during those nights I'll probably bounce a few off of you. My poems are mostly complaints about mundane things like small airplane seats, and sometimes I appear insane. (I assure you that I actually am)

Let me know which side of the room you want,

[NAME]

What is Meaningful to You?

My music activities and ensembles constitute a large part of my identity. On weekends, my friends and I, "the Okay String Quartet," perform medleys of traditional tunes at nursery homes and Asian festivals. We perform pieces that I arrange from Pachelbel's Canon rock to B Rossette Korean Drama soundtrack covers. Although it is abnormal for a Violist to lead a quartet, we find it easier to have me coordinate logistics (practices and sheet music) so that our Violins can focus on solos.These blends of musical styles and performance demeanors have taught me to use music to connect with audiences of various backgrounds. Despite all four of us being Allstate Orchestra participants, we perform pieces at lower difficulties so that we can spend more time messing around and improvising because our quartet was formed for fun.

In addition to my quartet, I also perform with our school's jazz band as an Upright Bassist. The vibe is entirely different from a concert band or an orchestra, and I enjoy being the steady beat giver of the group. Although I'm not out front leading the band as the horns do, my role managing the low notes helps to fill the room with sound and to provide a crucial foundation for

INSIDE STANFORD ADMISSIONS

the group. This group is important to me because it's taught me how to build off of a soloist's excitement and to overlay energies to create unique emotions.

What is the most significant challenge that society faces today?

Environmental unsustainability. Prioritization of individual profit over the collective good, leading to a resource lacking future. As exemplified by the tragedy of the commons problem, every level from international governments to local communities exploits the environment because they assume that others will fix their problems, leading to the free-rider problem.

How did you spend your last two summers?

Sophomore summer, I worked in an immunology lab and researched Myeloid Derived Suppressor Cells, a new subspecies of inflammatory cells, and their appearances in mice colon.

Last summer, I was a Science major at Georgia's Governor's Honors Program, and I taught myself the basics of the computer language R.

What historical moment or event do you wish you could have witnessed?

At first I wanted to travel to the Roaring Twenties and to Jay Gatsby's mansion to experience the vibrant jazz and the upbeat tap-dancing—to observe firsthand the culture of conspicuous consumption and the Dadaism movement—but then I realized that I'm not white, and that would be a questionable journey.

What five words best describe you?

Empathetic, Skeptical, Pragmatic, Analytical, Ambitious

When the choice is yours, what do you read, listen to, or watch?

Slam poetry, Postmodern Jukebox Jazz, WIRED, TedED riddles, BYU Vocal point, 2Cellos, Vsauce, The Pianoguys, Jeopardy, SoulPancake, Solfa, The New Yorker, Kurt Hugo Schneider, Narcos, Anna Karenina by Tolstoy, The Republic by Plato, The Prince by Machiavelli, The Three Body Problem by Cixin Liu, Cinda Williams Chima, John Flanagan

Name one thing you are looking forward to experiencing at Stanford.

The innovative spirit and the excitement that drips through every interaction at Stanford is something I look forward to experiencing. I want to connect with passionate people who do what they do because they like doing it, not because they're seeking a high salary.

Imagine you had an extra hour in the day—how would you spend that time?

I would pick up another student to tutor. Currently, I teach math, science, SAT reading and writing, violin, and bass classes to help with the bills. I've had to turn away students because I couldn't fit multiple lessons into my schedule, so I would probably start teaching piano again.

Reader 1

PE: nice PE about music. no significant evidence of depth of thought or noncogs. Sincere, light, open. Humility evident. An introspective, realistic writer.

Comment: Not sure if there is POE, but achievement while helping family is significant. Excellent grades/testing with evidence of SPIV and noncogs push file to emerge.

Reader 2

Strong WL/comp discussion for powerhouse gen1 scholar. Without stronger impact, not sure [NAME] will emerge.

Tags

Gen1, QBF

Reader 1 Scores	
Metric	**Score**
Test Rtg	1
HSR	2
Support	3
EC	2
SP-IV	2
Eval	2-

Reader 2 Scores	
Metric	**Score**
Test Rtg	1
HSR	3
Support	3
EC	3
SP-IV	2
Eval	2

Conclusion

That's it folks! We hope that, over the course of this book, reading about other people, you've learned a bit about yourself. We hope that you've gained some insight into the Stanford admissions process. And finally, we hope we've made applying a little less scary for you.

We wish you the best of luck, and we look forward to meeting you when we're on campus.

Made in the USA
Middletown, DE
24 September 2023